بِدَايَةُ العَابِدِ وَكِفَايَةُ الزَّاهِدِ

Bidāyat al-ʿĀbid wa Kifāyat al-Zāhid

Commencement of the Worshiper
& Sufficiency of the Ascetic

ʿAbd al-Raḥmān b. ʿAbd Allāh al-Baʿli
(1110-1192 H)

Translation & Annotation
by
John N. Starling, III

Edition 2.3, Ramaḍān 1440 | May 2019

ISBN: 978-0692960578

Contents

مَذْهَبُ أَحْمَدَ أَحْمَدُ مَذْهَبٍ

Aḥmad's school is the most praiseworthy.

Abū Ismāʿīl al-Anṣāri
396-481

Foreword

In the name of Allāh, the Most-Generous the Most-Merciful. All praise belongs to Allāh, the Lord of the worlds, and may peace and prayers be upon our Prophet Muḥammad, his family, companions, and all that follow them in the best manner until the Day of Judgment.

Seeking religious knowledge is from the most virtuous ways Muslims can spend their time. Accordingly, granting people access to it in a simple and easy manner, especially those who do not speak Arabic, is from the best of deeds.

The lofty aspirations of our virtuous brother Shaykh Abu Ibrāhīm John Starling, from the United States of America, has led to the English translation of Bidāyat al-ʿĀbid wa Kifāyat al-Zāhid by the Imām ʿAbd al-Raḥmān b. ʿAbd Allāh al-Baʿli al-Ḥanbalī. This is extremely important work due to the lack of translated Fiqh books, especially concise juristic manuals.

Shaykh Abu Ibrāhīm has studied this manual, coordinated through 'WhatsApp', and received an ijāzah from the penurious servant. I ask that Allāh bless his efforts and benefit the Muslims from his work.

Dr. Muṭlaq b. Jāsir b. Muṭlaq al-Jāsir
Department of Comparative Fiqh
Faculty of Sharia, University of Kuwait
Ramaḍān 25, 1438 H

Preface

The following is a dual language presentation of Imām al-Baʿli's, Bidāyat al-ʿĀbid wa Kifāyat al-Zāhid. I have relied upon the author's explanation as a primary reference during the translation process. On occasion, I have given precedence to Shaykh Dr. Muṭlaq al-Jāsir's commentary and corrections of the published text.

I have tried to make this manual as accessible to the reader as possible, while maintaining the codified nature of the original text. The untrained reader will require a qualified teacher to unlock its code. I have intentionally avoided adding additions, explanations between brackets, and footnotes unless I felt it necessary, such as with many of the chapter headings. My hope with this translation is to encourage students to learn Arabic as well as to acquaint themselves with the Ḥanbalī school, the style of the jurist, and revive the master/apprentice relationship in scholarship.

I would like to thank Shaykh Dr. Muṭlaq al-Jāsir for teaching me this text, writing the foreword, and for his service to Islām and the Ḥanbali school. I ask that Allāh reward him immensely and grant him success in this life and the next. I must also thank my good friend and colleague Shaykh Rashīd Aḥmadi for painstakingly reviewing the translation with me multiple times.

Many thanks are also extended to my mother-in-law, Umm ʿAbd Allāh for initial proofing and editing, as well as her lovely daughter, Umm Ibrāhīm, for her unwavering support. I ask that Allāh reward those involved and overlook any faults and mistakes.

Introduction to the Second Edition

After an unexpectedly positive reception of the first edition, I felt compelled to undertake a revision of the translation, which suffered from numerous typos, grammatical errors, and a handful of erroneous conclusions.

Besides merely correcting the above-mentioned flaws in the text, I decided to add further value to this edition by including numerous footnotes to define technical Islamic terms and clarify several extremely codified phrases. For the Arabic student, I have reviewed the original Arabic text for accuracy, comparing it with several primary resources, and added 90-95% of the diacritical marks.

For a more aesthetically pleasing presentation, I have reformatted the book so that the English translation is on the left side and the Arabic text is on the right.

I ask that Allāh accept and bless this effort and forgive me for any faults, as I do not expect that it is perfect.

I would like to thank everyone who sent constructive feedback on the first edition, especially Shaykh Majed Jarrar, whose suggestions were invaluable. May Allāh reward you immensely!

About the Author

The shaykh, jurist, scholar, and skilled Imām ʿAbd al-Raḥmān b. ʿAbd Allāh b. Aḥmad al-Ḥalabi al-Dimashqi al-Ḥanbali was born on 21, Jumādā al-Ūlā, 1110H in Baʿlabak. He was raised in a house filled with knowledge; his father, grandfather and great-grandfather were all revered scholars along with his older brothers Shaykh Muḥammad al-Ḥanbali and Shaykh Aḥmad the author of al-Rawḍ al-Nadā, the explanation of Kāfī al-Mubtadī.

After he reached the age of discernment, he began his study of the Qurʾān with his father, completing it by the age of 10. He then began seeking knowledge with his first teacher, Shaykh ʿAwwād al-Ḥanbali al-Nābulsi who taught him al-Ājrūmiyyah in Arabic grammar and Akhṣar al-Mukhtaṣarāt/The Supreme Synopsis in Fiqh. He studied with Shaykh 'Awwād for many years, gradually developing and maturing in his knowledge.

After his father passed away, he remained under the tutelage of his brother and scholar, Shaykh Abu al-Muwāhib al-Ḥanbali, for five years, learning Fiqh and Ḥadīth. He also studied with the scholar Abd al-Qadir al-Taghlibi al-Ḥanbali, author of Nayl al-Maʾārib, for 15 years, learning Ḥadīth, Fiqh, Arabic grammar, Inheritance, and Usūl. Upon the completion of his studies, he was granted a general ijāzah. He also attended the lessons of the scholar Shaykh Ismāʿīl al-Ajlūni, author of Kashf al-Khafāʾa, on Saḥīḥ al-Bukhāri under the Nasr Dome in the Umayyad Masjid for approximately nine years and was granted a general ijāzah. Later, he traveled to Aleppo and remained there studying Ḥadīth, Logic, Usūl, Grammar, and Rhetoric. He had numerous teachers and received many accolades from them, as well as ijāzahs. He also possessed the shortest chain of narration to Saḥīḥ al-Bukhāri, which was a mere 10 narrators.

Imām al-Baʿli was praised by many scholars and was known for seeking knowledge his entire life from his numerous teachers.

Al-Murādi said, "the shaykh, the scholar, the virtuous, the righteous, was a Faqīh, proficient in the Islamic Sciences; in particular, the various recitations..."

Ibn Badrān said, "He was a Faqīh, an expert, eloquent, a poet...". Shaykh ʿAbd al-Hayy al-Kettāni said, "The shaykh, the scholar, the reciter, and possessor of isnād...".

He authored numerous books which are noted below.

An abridgement of al-Jāmiʿ al-Ṣaghīr of al-Suyūti called Nūr al-Akhyār wa Rawḍ al-Abrār fī Ḥadīth al-Nabi al-Musṭafā al-Mukhtār which he confined to the ḥadīth transmitted by Imāms Aḥmad, al-Bukhāri, and Muslim.

An explanation of the previous book entitled, Fatḥ al-Sitār wa Kashf al-Mukhtār.

A concise manual of worship entitled Bidāyat al-ʿĀbid wa Kifāyat al-Zāhid.

An explanation of the previous book entitled, Bulūgh al-Qāṣid Jull al-Maqāṣid.

An explanation of Ibn Balbān's Akhṣar al-Mukhtaṣarāt entitled, Kashf al-Mukhadarāt wa Riyāḍ al-Muzhirāt.

A scholarly poem abridging al-Raḥbiyyah entitled, al-Durrat al-Maḍiyah fī Ikhtisār al-Raḥbiyyah.

An explanation of the previous poem entitled al-Fawaʾid al-Marḍiyyah.

A poem entitled Naẓm al-Ājrūmiyyah.

ʿAbd al-Raḥmān al-Baʿli remained in Aleppo with support from numerous righteous people who supplied him with a livable wage and whatever he needed to live until his passing in 1192H. May Allāh shower him with mercy.

Author's Introduction

In the name of Allāh the Most-Gracious, Most-Merciful. All praise belongs to Allāh who bestows understanding of the faith upon whom He wills from the servants and grants success in worship and veracity to those obedient to Him. We ask Allāh for eternal and continuous prayers and peace for our leader Muḥammad, the guide to the path of truth, for his family, his honorable leading and exemplary companions, and all who perfectly follow them until the Day of Return.

I have sought Allāh's guidance in authoring a beneficial and concise manual restricted to the acts of worship based on the jurisprudence of the highly regarded Imām Abū ʿAbdullāh Aḥmad b. Ḥanbal to encourage the disciple and grant access to those seeking benefit. I have called it, 'Bidāyat al-ʿĀbid wa Kifāyat al-Zāhid'. I request that Allāh accept it and to benefit everyone, both inquirer and inquired of, who busies themselves with it, for indeed He is the most generous in whom to place one's hope.

مُقَدِّمَةُ المُؤَلِّفِ

بِسْمِ اللَّهِ الرَّحْمَنِ الرَّحِيمِ، الحَمْدُ لِلَّهِ الَّذِي فَقَّهَ فِي دِينِهِ مَنْ شَاءَ مِنَ العِبَادِ، وَوَفَّقَ أَهَلَ طَاعَتِهِ لِلْعِبَادَةِ وَالسَّدَادِ، وَالصَّلَاةُ وَالسَّلَامُ عَلَى سَيِّدِنَا مُحَمَّدٍ الهَادِي إِلَى طَرِيقِ الرَّشَادِ، وَعَلَى آلِهِ وَأَصْحَابِهِ السَّادَةِ القَادَةِ الأَمْجَادِ، وَعَلَى تَابِعِيهِمْ بِإِحْسَانٍ صَلَاةً دَائِمَةً مُتَّصِلَةً إِلَى يَوْمِ المَعَادِ.

أَمَّا بَعْدُ فَقَدْ اسْتَخَرْتُ اللَّهَ فِي جَمْعِ مُخْتَصَرٍ مُفِيدٍ، مُقْتَصِرًا فِيهِ عَلَى العِبَادَاتِ تَرْغِيباً لِلْمُرِيدِ، وَتَقْرِيباً لِلْمُسْتَفِيدِ، فِي فِقْهِ الإِمَامِ المُبَجَّلِ، أَبِي عَبْدِ اللَّهِ أَحْمَدَ بْنِ مُحَمَّدٍ بْنِ حَنْبَلٍ، وَسَمَّيْتُهُ "بِدَايَةَ العَابِدِ وَكِفَايَةَ الزَّاهِدِ"، وَمِنَ اللَّهِ تَعَالَى أَرْتَجِي لَهُ القَبُولَ وَالنَّفْعَ لِكُلِّ مَنْ اشْتَغَلَ بِهِ مِنْ سَائِلٍ وَمَسْؤُولٍ، إِنَّهُ أَكْرَمُ مَأْمُولٍ.

Purification

It is the removal of a ḥadath[1] and elimination of a khabath[2].

Water is of three types: ṭahūr; ṭāhir; and najis.

Ṭahūr is what remains in its natural state. It is intrinsically pure and an abluent. It is categorically permissible to use.

Ṭāhir is what has greatly changed in color, taste, or odor due to a ṭāhir object. It is intrinsically pure, but not an abluent. It is permissible to use, except to remove a ḥadath or a khabath.

Najis[3] is what has changed due to najāsah[4], except on the location being purified. It is categorically impermissible to use, unless in dire need[5].

An abundant amount is two qullahs or more and a meager amount is lesser than that. They are equivalent to 107.7 Damascus pounds or whatever is comparable[6].

Ṭāhir vessels are permissible to keep and use, as long as they are neither gold nor silver.

---

[1] A state which prevents one from prayer, etc.

[2] Synonym of najāsah.

[3] The opposite of ṭāhir.

[4] Every substance which is impermissible to handle, not due to it being sacred, regarded as filthy, or it being harmful to the body or mind. It is also defined as every substance which requires purification.

[5] Such as drinking it to remove a lodged morsel of food to prevent choking to death.

[6] Approximately 191 liters or 50 US liquid gallons.

كِتَابُ الطَّهَارَةِ

وَهِيَ ارْتِفَاعُ الحَدَثِ وَزَوَالُ الخَبَثِ.

وَالمِيَاهُ ثَلاثَةٌ: طَهُورٌ، وَطَاهِرٌ، وَنَجِسٌ.

فَالطَّهُورُ: هُوَ البَاقِي عَلَى خِلْقَتِهِ طَهُورٌ فِي نَفْسِهِ مُطَهِّرٌ لِغَيْرِهِ، يَجُوزُ اسْتِعْمَالُهُ مُطْلَقاً.

وَالطَّاهِرُ: مَا تَغَيَّرَ كَثِيرٌ مِن لَوْنِهِ أَوْ طَعْمِهِ أَوْ رِيحِهِ بِطَاهِرٍ، وَهُوَ طَاهِرٌ فِي نَفْسِهِ غَيْرُ مُطَهِّرٍ لِغَيْرِهِ، يَجُوزُ اسْتِعْمَالُهُ فِي غَيْرِ رَفْعِ حَدَثٍ وَزَوَالِ خَبَثٍ.

وَالنَّجِسُ: مَا تَغَيَّرَ بِنَجَاسَةٍ فِي غَيْرِ مَحَلِّ تَطْهِيرٍ، وَيَحْرُمُ اسْتِعْمَالُهُ مُطْلَقاً إِلَّا لِضَرُورَةٍ.

وَالكَثِيرُ قُلَّتَانِ فَأَكْثَرُ، وَاليَسِيرُ مَا دُونَهُمَا، وَهُمَا: مِائَةُ رِطْلٍ وَسَبْعَةُ أَرْطَالٍ وَسُبُعُ رِطْلٍ بِالدِّمَشْقِيِّ وَمَا وَافَقَهُ.

وَكُلُّ إِنَاءٍ طَاهِرٍ يُبَاحُ اتِّخَاذُهُ وَاسْتِعْمَالُهُ غَيْرَ ذَهَبٍ وَفِضَّةٍ.

Istinjā', Istijmār, Manners of the Restroom

Istinjā' is the act of removing whatever comes out of a tract with water or stone, etc. It is obligated due to everything that comes out except flatulence, anything ṭāhir, or something unsoiled.

Istijmār is not valid unless performed with something ṭāhir, permissible, dry, and cleansing. Cleaning with a stone, etc. is concluded when nothing remains except for traces only removable by water.

The following are prerequisites: that it be made with three wipes or more which cleanse; the excrement must not surpass its normal location; and if water is used, it must completely clean the area, the assumption of which is sufficient.

It is impermissible to use manure, bone, or food, including animal feed. Neither wuḍū' nor tayammum are valid when made before it.

It is impermissible to: linger longer than one's pressing need; defecate in water; defecate or urinate in a watering place, on a traversed path, in used shade, or under a fruit bearing tree of harvest; or to face or turn one's back to the qiblah[7] in open space.

---

[7] The direction of prayer.

فَصْلٌ

وَالاسْتِنْجَاءُ إِزَالَةُ مَا خَرَجَ مِنْ سَبِيلٍ بِمَاءٍ أَوْ حَجَرٍ وَنَحْوِهِ، وَهُوَ وَاجِبٌ مِنْ كُلِّ خَارِجٍ إِلَّا الرِّيحَ وَالطَّاهِرَ وَغَيْرَ الْمُلَوَّثِ.

وَلَا يَصِحُّ الاسْتِجْمَارُ إِلَّا بِطَاهِرٍ مُبَاحٍ يَابِسٍ مُنْقٍ، فَالإِنْقَاءُ بِحَجَرٍ وَنَحْوِهِ أَنْ يَبْقَى أَثَرٌ لَا يُزِيلُهُ إِلَّا الْمَاءُ.

وَشُرِطَ لَهُ: ثَلَاثُ مَسْحَاتٍ فَأَكْثَرُ مُنْقِيَةٍ، وَعَدَمُ تَعَدِّي خَارِجٍ مَوْضِعَ الْعَادَةِ، وَبِمَاءٍ عَوْدُ الْمَحَلِّ كَمَا كَانَ، وَظَنُّهُ كَافٍ. وَحَرُمَ بِرَوْثٍ وَعَظْمٍ وَطَعَامٍ وَلَوْ لِبَهِيمَةٍ، وَلَا يَصِحُّ وُضُوءٌ وَلَا تَيَمُّمٌ قَبْلَهُ.

وَحَرُمَ لَبْثٌ فَوْقَ قَدْرِ حَاجَتِهِ، وَتَغَوُّطُهُ بِمَاءٍ، وَبَوْلُهُ وَتَغَوُّطُهُ بِمَرْوَةٍ وَبِطَرِيقٍ مَسْلُوكٍ، وَظِلٍّ نَافِعٍ، وَتَحْتَ شَجَرَةٍ عَلَيْهَا ثَمَرٌ يُقْصَدُ، وَاسْتِقْبَالُ قِبْلَةٍ وَاسْتِدْبَارُهَا بِفَضَاءٍ.

Personal Hygiene

The siwāk[8] is categorically recommended, except after the zawāl[9], which is disliked for someone fasting. Before the zawāl, it is permissible with a moist stick, though preferred with a dry one. Whoever uses something besides a stick has not conformed to the sunnah.

It is emphasized before: prayer; recitation; when making wuḍū'; waking from sleep; entering the masjid; due to a change of breath; etc.

It is recommended to do the following: begin with the right side for siwāk, purification, and all affairs; use oil and kuḥl[10]; look in the mirror; apply perfume; shave the pubic region; trim the mustache[11]; cut the nails; and pluck the armpits.

Though early childhood is best, it is obligatory to circumcise[12] both male and female at the age of puberty.

---

[8] A traditional toothbrush fashioned from the Arāk tree (Salvadora Persica) containing antibacterial qualities which may help control the formation and activity of dental plaque.

[9] When the shadow appears to the east of its object i.e. moments after midday.

[10] A medicinal eye-liner traditionally made from stibnite (Sb_2S_3).

[11] It is recommended to let the beard grow without trimming any of it... 'so long as it's lengthiness is not unpleasant'. It is impermissible to shave it but not sinful to trim whatever exceeds a fist length.

[12] Circumcision refers to both the removal of a male's foreskin and the extra skin above a woman's vaginal-opening resembling a cockscomb e.g. partial hoodectomy, which should not be removed entirely and if health risks are too high, the obligation is voided.

فَصْلٌ

وَالسِّوَاكُ مَسْنُونٌ مُطْلَقاً، إِلَّا لِصَائِمٍ بَعْدَ الزَّوَالِ فَيُكْرَهُ، وَيُبَاحُ قَبْلَهُ بِعُودٍ رَطْبٍ، وَيُسْتَحَبُّ بِيَابِسٍ، وَلَمْ يُصِبِ السُّنَّةَ مَنْ اسْتَاكَ بِغَيْرِ عُودٍ.

وَيَتَأَكَّدُ عِنْدَ صَلَاةٍ وَقِرَاءَةٍ وَوُضُوءٍ، وَانْتِبَاهٍ مِنْ نَوْمٍ، وَدُخُولِ مَسْجِدٍ وَتَغَيُّرِ رَائِحَةِ فَمٍ وَنَحْوِهِ.

وَسُنَّ: بُدَاءَةٌ بِالأَيْمَنِ فِي سِوَاكٍ وَطُهُورٍ وَشَأْنِهِ كُلِّهِ، وَادِّهَانٌ،وَاكْتِحَالٌ، وَنَظَرٌ فِي مِرْآةٍ، وَتَطَيُّبٌ، وَاسْتِحْدَادٌ، وَحَفُّ شَارِبٍ، وَتَقْلِيمُ ظُفْرٍ، وَنَتْفُ إِبْطٍ.

وَيَجِبُ خِتَانُ ذَكَرٍ وَأُنْثَى عِنْدَ بُلُوغٍ، وَزَمَنَ صِغَرٍ أَفْضَلُ.

Wuḍū'

Wuḍū' is the application of ṭahūr water on four designated body parts in a specific manner. Mentioning Allāh's name for it, ghusl, tayammum, washing the hands after waking from a night's sleep that has invalidated wuḍū', and washing the deceased is obligatory. It is obligatory to wash both hands three times when waking from a night's sleep, after making an intention and mentioning Allāh's name.

Wuḍū' has eight prerequisites, they are: cessation of what obligates it; intention, a prerequisite for every form of purification except eliminating khabath, etc.; Islām; sanity; discernment; permissible ṭahūr water; removal of what prohibits it; and istinjā'.

It has six obligations, they are: washing the face (which includes the mouth and nose); washing the hands, including the elbows; wiping the entire head, including the ears; washing both feet, including the ankles; sequence; and continuity (both of which are not required for ghusl).

فَصْلٌ

وَالْوُضُوءُ اسْتِعْمَالُ مَاءٍ طَهُورٍ فِي الْأَعْضَاءِ الْأَرْبَعَةِ عَلَى صِفَةٍ مَخْصُوصَةٍ، وَالتَّسْمِيَةُ وَاجِبَةٌ فِيهِ، وَفِي غُسْلٍ، وَتَيَمُّمٍ، وَغَسْلِ يَدَيْ قَائِمٍ مِنْ نَوْمِ لَيْلٍ نَاقِضٍ لِوُضُوءٍ، وَغَسْلِ مَيِّتٍ، وَيَجِبُ غَسْلُ يَدَيِ الْقَائِمِ مِنْ نَوْمِ اللَّيْلِ ثَلَاثًا بِنِيَّةٍ وَتَسْمِيَةٍ.

وَشُرُوطُ الْوُضُوءِ ثَمَانِيَةٌ: انْقِطَاعُ مَا يُوجِبُهُ، وَالنِّيَّةُ، وَهِيَ شَرْطٌ لِكُلِّ طَهَارَةٍ شَرْعِيَّةٍ غَيْرَ إِزَالَةِ خَبَثٍ وَنَحْوِهَا، وَالْإِسْلَامُ، وَالْعَقْلُ، وَالتَّمْيِيزُ، وَالْمَاءُ الطَّهُورُ الْمُبَاحُ، وَإِزَالَةُ مَا يَمْنَعُ وُصُولَهُ، وَالِاسْتِنْجَاءُ.

وَفُرُوضُهُ سِتَّةٌ: غَسْلُ الْوَجْهِ، وَمِنْهُ فَمٌ وَأَنْفٌ، وَغَسْلُ الْيَدَيْنِ مَعَ الْمِرْفَقَيْنِ، وَمَسْحُ الرَّأْسِ كُلِّهِ وَمِنْهُ الْأُذُنَانِ، وَغَسْلُ الرِّجْلَيْنِ مَعَ الْكَعْبَيْنِ، وَتَرْتِيبٌ، وَمُوَالَاةٌ، وَيَسْقُطَانِ مَعَ غُسْلٍ.

Wiping the Khuff

It is permitted to wipe over the khuffs, etc., if the following seven prerequisites are met: wearing them after a complete purification with water; concealing the obligatory area; having the ability to walk (as per custom) in them; that they be independently fixed; permissible; ṭāhir; and that they not reveal the skin. After wearing them, both the resident and the traveler on a sinful journey are to wipe after a ḥadath for a day and a night. The traveler on a journey, which is not sinful in nature, of sufficient distance to shorten prayer is to wipe for three days and their nights. If someone were to wipe during travel and then settle, as a resident and then travel, or doubted when the wiping period began, they are not to exceed the wiping period of a resident.

It is permitted to wipe over a cast, which does not exceed the required size, if worn after purification. If it does exceed that, or was put on while impure, it must be removed. Due to formidable harm, tayammum is to be made along with wiping that which exceeds the required size and was worn in a state of purity.

If a portion of an obligatory part is revealed, something which necessitates ghusl occurs, or the time period expires, wuḍū᾽ is invalidated.

فَصْلٌ

يَجُوزُ المَسْحُ عَلَى الخُفَّيْنِ وَنَحوِهِمَا بِسَبْعَةِ شُرُوطٍ: لُبْسُهُمَا بَعْدَ كَمَالِ طَهَارَةٍ بِمَاءٍ، وَسَتْرُهُمَا لِمَحَلِّ فَرْضٍ، وإمْكَانُ مَشْيٍ بِهِمَا عُرْفاً، وثُبُوتُهُمَا بِنَفْسِهِمَا، وَإِبَاحَتُهُمَا، وَطَهَارَةُ عَيْنِهِمَا، وَعَدَمُ وَصْفِهِمَا البَشَرَةَ. فَيَمْسَحُ مُقِيمٌ وَعَاصٍ بِسَفَرِهِ مِنْ حَدَثٍ بَعْدَ لُبْسٍ يوماً وَلَيلَةً، وَمُسَافِرٌ سَفَرَ قَصْرٍ لَمْ يَعْصِ بِهِ ثَلاثَةً بِلَيَالِيهِنَّ، فَلَوْ مَسَحَ فِي سَفَرٍ ثُمَّ أَقَامَ، أَوْ فِي حَضَرٍ ثُمَّ سَافَرَ، أَوْ شَكَّ فِي ابْتِدَاءِ المَسْحِ لَمْ يَزِدْ عَلَى مَسْحِ مُقِيمٍ.

وَيَجُوزُ المَسْحُ عَلَى جَبِيرَةٍ إِنْ كَانَ وَضَعَهَا عَلَى طَهَارَةٍ وَلَمْ تُجَاوِزْ قَدْرَ الحَاجَةِ، وَإِنْ جَاوَزَتْهُ أَوْ كَانَ وَضَعَهَا عَلَى غَيْرِ طَهَارَةٍ وَجَبَ نَزْعُهَا، فَإِنْ خَافَ ضَرَراً تَيَمَّمَ مَعَ مَسْحِ مَوْضُوعَةٍ عَلَى طَهَارَةٍ مُجَاوِزَةٍ مَحَلِّ الحَاجَةِ.

وَإِنْ ظَهَرَ بَعْضُ مَحَلِّ فَرْضٍ أَوْ حَصَلَ مَا يُوجِبُ الغُسْلَ أَوْ انْقَضَتْ المُدَّةُ بَطَلَ الوُضُوءُ.

Invalidators of Wuḍū'

There are eight invalidators of wuḍū' which are: excretion of anything from a tract, of urine or feces from the rest of the body (be it a lot or a little); or excretion of other things such as vomit or blood if considered abundant (relative to each person's own view); loss of consciousness (except the dozing of someone standing or sitting); washing the deceased or a portion thereof; eating camel meat, even if raw, (a cause which is purely devotional, as its other parts do not invalidate it e.g. drinking its milk or meat stock); touching an attached human sex organ[16] or anus, even if deceased, with the hand (excluding the testicles and the location of a severed sex organ); the desirous touch of the opposite gender without a barrier (even via extra appendage to another); and apostasy.

Everything which requires ghusl requires wuḍū', except death, which only requires ghusl; wuḍū' is recommended. It is not invalidated due to impermissible speech, or the removal of hair, nails, etc. Whoever doubts the performance of purification or the occurrence of a ḥadath, even while not in prayer, is to act upon what they are certain of.

---

[16] Be it either the penis of a man or the vaginal opening of a woman.

فَصْلٌ

نَوَاقِضُ الوُضُوءِ ثَمَانِيَةٌ: خَارِجٌ مِنْ سَبِيلٍ مُطْلَقاً، وَخُرُوجُ بَوْلٍ أَوْ غَائِطٍ مِنْ بَاقِي البَدَنِ قَلَّ أَو كَثُرَ أَوْ غَيْرِهِمَا كَقَيْءٍ أَوْ دَمٍ إِنْ فَحُشَ فِي نَفْسِ كُلِّ أَحَدٍ بِحَسَبِهِ، وَزَوَالُ عَقْلٍ إِلَّا يَسِيرَ نَوْمٍ مِنْ قَائِمٍ أَوْ جَالِسٍ، وَغُسْلُ مَيِّتٍ أَوْ بَعْضِهِ، وَأَكْلُ لَحْمِ إِبِلٍ، وَلَو نَيْئاً تَعَبُّداً، فَلَا نَقْضَ بِبَقِيَّةِ أَجْزَائِهَا، وَشُرْبِ لَبَنِهَا وَمَرَقِ لَحْمِهَا، وَمَسُّ فَرْجِ آدَمِيٍّ مُتَّصِلٍ أَوْ حَلْقَةِ دُبُرِهِ وَلَوْ مَيِّتاً بِيَدِهِ لَا مَسُّ الخِصْيَتَيْنِ، وَلَا مَحَلُّ الفَرْجِ البَائِنِ، وَلَمْسُ ذَكَرٍ أَوْ أُنْثَى الآخَرَ لِشَهْوَةٍ بِلَا حَائِلٍ، وَلَوْ بِزَائِدٍ لِزَائِدٍ، وَالرِّدَّةُ.

وَكُلُّ مَا أَوْجَبَ غُسْلاً أَوْجَبَ وُضُوءًا غَيْرَ مَوْتٍ؛ فَإِنَّه يُوجِبُ الغُسْلَ لَا الوُضُوءَ، بَلْ يُسَنُّ، وَلَا نَقْضَ بِكَلَامٍ مُحَرَّمٍ، وَلَا بِإِزَالَةِ شَعْرٍ وَظُفْرٍ وَنَحْوِهِمَا، وَمَنْ شَكَّ فِي طَهَارَةٍ أَوْ حَدَثٍ وَلَوْ فِي غَيْرِ صَلَاةٍ بَنَى عَلَى يَقِينِهِ.

Ghusl

There are seven mandatory causes for ghusl[17], which include the following: secretion of orgasmic fluid (Ghusl is obligatory even if its mere secretion is sensed and ejaculation is prevented[18]. If ghusl is thus performed and then it apathetically discharges, it is not repeated); its ejaculation—even if bloody[19]—from its location (with consideration given to an orgasm of someone not sleeping, etc.); the insertion of a primary male glans, or its equivalent, into a primary sexual opening including an anus (even that of an animal or corpse) and of someone with whom intercourse is performed, even while asleep; acceptance of Islām by a disbeliever (even if they were an apostate and/or have done nothing which requires ghusl while in the state of disbelief); the excretion of menstrual or postpartum blood (it is not required for a delivery absent of bleeding); and death (a cause for which ghusl is purely devotional) of other than the martyred in battle or the wrongly killed.

The prayer place for 'Eid (not for funeral prayers) is considered a masjid in which seeking commercial profit is prohibited.

---

[17] The usage of ṭahūr water on the entire body in a specific manner.

[18] Like retrograde ejaculation.

[19] Appearing red in color.

فَصْلٌ

مُوجِبَاتُ الغُسْلِ سَبْعَةٌ: انْتِقَالُ مَنِيٍّ، فَلَوْ أَحَسَّ بِانْتِقَالِهِ فَحَبَسَهُ فَلَمْ يَخْرُجْ وَجَبَ الغُسْلُ، فَلَوْ اغْتَسَلَ لَهُ ثُمَّ خَرَجَ بِلَا لَذَّةٍ لَمْ يُعِدْهُ، وَخُرُوجُهُ مِنْ مَخْرَجِهِ وَلَوْ دَماً، وَتُعْتَبَرُ لَذَّةٌ فِي غَيْرِ نَائِمٍ وَنَحْوِهِ. وَتَغْيِيبُ حَشَفَةٍ أَصْلِيَّةٍ أَوْ قَدْرِهَا فِي فَرْجٍ أَصْلِيٍّ وَلَوْ دُبُراً لِبَهِيمَةٍ أَوْ مَيِّتٍ مِمَّنْ يُجَامِعُ مِثْلُهُ وَلَوْ نَائِماً، وَإِسْلَامُ كَافِرٍ، وَلَوْ مُرْتَدّاً أَوْ لَمْ يُوجَدْ مِنْهُ فِي كُفْرِهِ مَا يُوجِبُهُ، وَخُرُوجُ حَيْضٍ، وَخُرُوجُ دَمِ نِفَاسٍ، فَلَا يَجِبُ بِوِلَادَةٍ عَرَتْ عَنْهُ، وَمَوْتٌ تَعَبُّداً غَيْرَ شَهِيدِ مَعْرَكَةٍ وَمَقْتُولٍ ظُلْماً.

وَمُصَلَّى العِيدِ لَا الجَنَائِزِ مَسْجِدٌ، وَيَحْرُمُ تَكَسُّبٌ بِصَنْعَةٍ فِيهِ.

Prerequisites of Ghusl

The seven prerequisites of ghusl are: cessation of what requires it; intention; Islām; sanity; discernment; purifying permissible water; and removal of whatever prevents its contact. It is obligatory that water wet the entire body, along with the inside of the mouth and nose, as well as what appears of a woman's vulva when she sits to relieve herself. Assumption is sufficient for completeness. Whoever intends either a recommended or an obligatory ghusl will be sufficed for the other.

Sleeping while sexually impure is disliked without wuḍū'. Constructing bath-houses, selling and renting them, reciting in them, and giving greetings of peace in them is also disliked; but not dhikr. It is permissible to enter them while clothed and secure from the occurrence of something impermissible, disliked if otherwise feared, and impermissible if known or if a woman were to enter without justification.

فَصْلٌ

وَشُرُوطُ الغُسْلِ سَبْعَةٌ: انْقِطَاعُ مَا يُوجِبُهُ، وَالنِّيَّةُ، وَالإِسْلَامُ، وَالعَقْلُ، وَالتَّمْيِيزُ، وَالمَاءُ الطَّهُورُ المُبَاحُ، وَإِزَالَةُ مَا يَمْنَعُ وُصُولَهُ. وَفَرْضُهُ أَنْ يَعُمَّ بِالمَاءِ جَمِيعَ بَدَنِهِ وَدَاخِلَ فَمِهِ وَأَنْفِهِ حَتَّى مَا يَظْهَرُ مِنْ فَرْجِ امْرَأَةٍ عِنْدَ قُعُودِهَا لِحَاجَتِهَا، وَيَكْفِي الظَّنُّ فِي الإِسْبَاغِ، وَمَنْ نَوَى غُسْلاً مَسْنُوناً أَوْ وَاجِباً أَجْزَأَ عَنِ الآخَرِ.

وَكُرِهَ نَوْمُ جُنُبٍ بِلَا وُضُوءٍ، وَيُكْرَهُ بِنَاءُ الحَمَّامِ وَبَيْعُهُ وَإِجَارَتُهُ وَالقِرَاءَةُ فِيهِ، وَالسَّلَامُ لَا الذِّكْرُ، وَدُخُولُهُ بِسُتْرَةٍ مَعَ أَمْنِ الوُقُوعِ فِي مُحَرَّمٍ مُبَاحٌ، وَإِنْ خِيفَ كُرِهَ، وَإِنْ عَلِمَ أَوْ دَخَلَتْهُ أُنْثَى بِلَا عُذْرٍ حَرُمَ.

Tayammum

Tayammum is a specific application of earth on the face and hands as a replacement for water-based purification due to a legal inability, except for filth not found on the body or remaining in the masjid due to a need.

Its three prerequisites are: entrance of the prayer time; absence of water due to it being withheld, etc.; or due to fear of either physical or financial harm resulting from its usage, etc. Whoever finds water which is not sufficient for purification is obliged to use it and then perform tayammum[20]. It is made with ṭahūr permissible unfired earth that has dust which sticks to the hand. In its absence, one is to pray what is required, as they are, not adding more than what is sufficient and is not obliged to repeat it.

Its obligations include: wiping the face and the hands to the wrists; both sequence and continuity for a minor ḥadath, i.e. equivalent to wuḍū'; and specifying an intention legalizing what tayammum is being performed for of either ḥadath or najāsah. An intent for one is not sufficient for the other, however an intention for both is sufficient.

It is invalidated by the following: whatever invalidates wuḍū'; the time expiring; the presence of water (if tayammum was performed due to its absence); the termination of what permitted it; or the removal of what was wiped over.

---

[20] All available water must be exhausted, even if for a partial purification, before tayummum can be made.

فَصْلٌ

التَيَمُّمُ اسْتِعْمَالُ تُرَابٍ مَخْصُوصٍ لِوَجْهٍ وَيَدَيْنِ بَدَلُ طَهَارَةِ ماءٍ لِكُلِّ مَا يُفْعَلُ بِهِ عِنْدَ عَجْزٍ عَنْهُ شَرْعاً سِوَى نَجَاسَةٍ عَلَى غيرِ بَدَنٍ، وَلُبْثٍ بِمَسْجِدٍ لِحاجَةٍ.

وَشُرُوطُهُ ثَلاثَةٌ: دُخُولُ وَقْتِ الصَّلاةِ، وَتَعَذُّرُ المَاءِ لِحَبْسِهِ عَنْهُ وَنَحْوِهِ أَوْ لِخَوْفِهِ بِطَلَبِهِ أَوْ اسْتِعْمَالِهِ ضَرَراً بِبَدَنِهِ أَوْ مَالِهِ أَوْ غَيْرِهِمَا، وَمَنْ وَجَدَ مَاءً لَا يَكْفِي طَهَارَتَهُ اسْتَعْمَلَهُ وُجُوباً ثُمَّ تَيَمَّمَ، وَأَنْ يَكُونَ بِتُرَابٍ طَهُورٍ مُبَاحٍ غَيْرِ مُحْتَرِقٍ لَهُ غُبَارٌ يَعْلَقُ بِاليَدِ، فَإِنْ لَمْ يَجِدْ ذَلِكَ صَلَّى الفَرْضَ فَقَطْ عَلَى حَسَبِ حَالِهِ، وَلَا يَزِيدُ فِي صَلَاتِهِ عَلَى مُجْزِئٍ، وَلَا إِعَادَةَ عَلَيْهِ.

وَفُرُوضُهُ: مَسْحُ وَجْهِهِ، وَيَدَيْهِ إِلَى كُوعَيْهِ، وَتَرْتِيبٌ، وَمُوَالَاةٌ لِحَدَثٍ أَصْغَرَ، وَهِيَ بِقَدْرِ مَا فِي وُضُوءٍ، وَتَعْيِينُ نِيَّةِ اسْتِبَاحَةِ ما يَتَيَمَّمُ لَهُ مِنْ حَدَثٍ أَوْ نَجَاسَةٍ، فَلا تَكْفِي نِيَّةُ أَحَدِهِمَا عَنْ الآخَرِ، وَإِنْ نَوَاهُمَا أَجْزَأَ.

وَيُبْطِلُهُ ما يُبْطِلُ الوُضُوءَ، وَخُرُوجُ الوَقْتِ، وَوُجودُ المَاءِ إِنْ تَيَمَّمَ لِفَقْدِهِ، وَزَوَالُ المُبِيحِ لَهُ، وَخَلْعُ مَا يُمْسَحُ عَلَيْهِ.

Removal of Najāsah

Seven washes are required for everything contaminated by najāsah so long as they cleanse it. If not, then it is washed until purified with ṭahūr water coupled with scratching and scrubbing if needed (as long as the location is not damaged) and wringing absorbent material (outside of the water source) after every wash if possible. One of the washes must be done with ṭahūr earth if the soiled object was contaminated by a dog or a swine. A remaining taste is detrimental, but not a color, smell, or both if difficult to remove. It is sufficient to douse the urine of a baby boy (who has yet to eat food due to craving) with water until soaked. Rocks, basins, and land which have been soiled by liquid, even that of a dog or a swine, are to be sprayed with an abundant amount of water or until its color and smell are removed, as long as it is not impossible to remove one or the other. If the water is still present i.e. on the boy's urine, land, etc., they become purified even with the presence of the water.

Land is not purified by the sun, wind, or due to drying. Najāsah is not purified with fire; if so, its ash is najis. Alcohol is purified when it naturally turns to vinegar or due to moving it without intending acetification. Its container is similar[21]. If najāsah is concealed, it must be washed until it has surely been properly cleaned.

[21] The container takes the same ruling as the alcohol it holds i.e. if it becomes ṭāhir, the container becomes ṭāhir and vice versa.

فَصْلٌ

يُشْتَرَطُ لِكُلِّ مُتَنَجِّسٍ سَبْعُ غَسَلَاتٍ إِنْ أَنْقَتْ، وَإِلَّا فَحَتَّى تُنْقَى بِمَاءٍ طَهُورٍ مَعَ حَتِّ وَقَرْصٍ لِحَاجَةٍ، إِنْ لَمْ يَتَضَرَّرِ الْمَحَلُّ، وَعَصْرٍ مَعَ إِمْكَانٍ فِيمَا تَشَرَّبَ كُلَّ مَرَّةٍ خَارِجَ الْمَاءِ، وَكَوْنِ إِحْدَاهَا فِي مُتَنَجِّسٍ بِكَلْبٍ أَوْ خِنْزِيرٍ بِتُرَابٍ طَهُورٍ. وَيَضُرُّ بَقَاءُ طَعْمٍ لَا لَوْنٍ أَوْ رِيحٍ أَوْ هُمَا عَجْزاً. وَيُجْزِئُ فِي بَوْلِ غُلَامٍ لَمْ يَأْكُلْ طَعَاماً لِشَهْوَةٍ نَضْحُهُ، وَهُوَ غَمْرُهُ بِمَاءٍ، وَفِي نَحْوِ صَخْرٍ وَأَحْوَاضٍ وَأَرْضٍ تَنَجَّسَتْ بِمَائِعٍ، وَلَوْ مِنْ كَلْبٍ أَوْ خِنْزِيرٍ مُكَاثَرَتُهُمَا بِمَاءٍ حَتَّى يَذْهَبَ لَوْنُ النَّجَاسَةِ وَرِيحُهَا، مَا لَمْ يَعْجَزْ عَنْ إِذْهَابِهِمَا أَوْ إِذْهَابِ أَحَدِهِمَا، وَلَوْ لَمْ يَزُلِ الْمَاءُ فِيهِمَا أَيْ فِي بَوْلِ الْغُلَامِ وَفِي الْأَرْضِ وَنَحْوِهَا، فَيَطْهُرَانِ مَعَ بَقَاءِ الْمَاءِ عَلَيْهِمَا.

وَلَا تَطْهُرُ أَرْضٌ بِشَمْسٍ وَرِيحٍ وَجَفَافٍ، وَلَا نَجَاسَةٌ بِنَارٍ فَرَمَادُهَا نَجِسٌ. وَتَطْهُرُ خَمْرَةٌ انْقَلَبَتْ خَلّاً بِنَفْسِهَا أَوْ بِنَقْلٍ لَا لِقَصْدِ التَّخْلِيلِ، وَدَنُّهَا مِثْلُهَا، وَإِنْ خَفِيَتْ نَجَاسَةٌ غَسَلَ حَتَّى يَتَيَقَّنَ غَسْلَهَا.

Various Impurities

Liquid intoxicants, as well as birds and beasts (that are inedible and physically larger than a cat), are najis. Every carcass, besides humans, fish, and locusts, is najis. A small amount, per custom, of dirt from the roadways, which is known to be najis, is overlooked; otherwise it is ṭāhir[22].

The leftovers of a ṭāhir animal are not disliked i.e. their excess food and drink, except for that of non-sequestered chickens and mice. If a cat, etc., or a child were to eat najāsah and then drink from a small amount of water, it would be considered ṭāhir—even if before leaving.

[22] Because it is unknown to be najis.

فَصْلٌ

الْمُسْكِرُ الْمَائِعُ وَمَا لَا يُؤْكَلُ مِنَ الطَّيْرِ وَالْبَهَائِمِ مِمَّا فَوْقَ الْهِرِّ خِلْقَةً نَجِسٌ، وَكُلُّ مَيْتَةٍ نَجِسَةٌ غَيْرَ مَيْتَةِ الْآدَمِيِّ وَالسَّمَكِ وَالْجَرَادِ. وَيُعْفَى عَنْ يَسِيرِ طِينِ شَارِعٍ عُرْفاً إِنْ عُلِمَتْ نَجَاسَتُهُ وَإِلَّا فَهُوَ طَاهِرٌ.

وَلَا يُكْرَهُ سُؤْرُ حَيَوَانٍ طَاهِرٍ، وَهُوَ فَضْلَةُ طَعَامِهِ وَشَرَابِهِ غَيْرَ دَجَاجَةٍ مُخَلَّاةٍ وَفَأْرٍ، وَلَوْ أَكَلَ هِرٌّ وَنَحْوُهُ أَوْ طِفْلٌ نَجَاسَةً ثُمَّ شَرِبَ وَلَوْ قَبْلَ أَنْ يَغِيبَ مِنْ مَاءٍ يَسِيرٍ فَطَهُورٌ.

Blood of Women

The earliest age of menstruation is nine and the latest is 50. A pregnant woman does not menstruate. Its shortest period is one day and night and the longest is 15 days; most of the time it is six or seven. The shortest period of purity between two menstrual cycles is 13 days; most of the time it is the remainder of the month. There is no limit on how long it can be.

It is impermissible for her to perform prayer (which does not have to be made up), to fast (which must be made up), or to have intercourse with her (which requires one or one-half[23] dinār as an expiation[24]); other intimate acts are however permitted.

Postpartum bleeding has no limit on its shortest duration; its maximum is 40 days. It is ruled as such when whatever is delivered possesses human characteristics. Becoming clean during its duration is considered purity; intercourse during it is disliked. It is treated like menstruation in its rulings except for both the marital waiting period and maturity.

[23] The right to choose either one dinār or a half is like the choice of a traveler between completing the prayer or shortening it.

[24] It is required from both participating parties.

فَصْلٌ

وَأَقَلُّ سِنِّ حَيْضٍ تَمَامُ تِسْعِ سِنِينَ، وَأَكْثَرُهُ خَمْسُونَ سَنَةً وَالْحَامِلُ لَا تَحِيضُ. وَأَقَلُّهُ يَوْمٌ وَلَيْلَةٌ، وَأَكْثَرُهُ خَمْسَةَ عَشَرَ يَوْماً، وَغَالِبُهُ سِتٌّ أَوْ سَبْعٌ. وَأَقَلُّ الطُّهْرِ بَيْنَ الْحَيْضَتَيْنِ ثَلَاثَةَ عَشَرَ يَوْماً، وَغَالِبُهُ بَقِيَّةُ الشَّهْرِ، وَلَا حَدَّ لِأَكْثَرِهِ.

وَيَحْرُمُ عَلَيْهَا فِعْلُ صَلَاةٍ، وَلَا تَقْضِيهَا، وَفِعْلُ صَوْمٍ وَتَقْضِيهِ، وَوَطْؤُهَا فِي فَرْجٍ، وَيَجِبُ فِيهِ دِينَارٌ أَوْ نِصْفُهُ كَفَّارَةً، وَتُبَاحُ الْمُبَاشَرَةُ فِيمَا دُونَهُ.

وَالنِّفَاسُ لَا حَدَّ لِأَقَلِّهِ، وَأَكْثَرُهُ أَرْبَعُونَ يَوْماً، وَيَثْبُتُ حُكْمُهُ بِوَضْعِ مَا يَتَبَيَّنُ فِيهِ خَلْقُ الْإِنْسَانِ، وَالنَّقَاءُ زَمَنُهُ طُهْرٌ، وَيُكْرَهُ الْوَطْءُ فِيهِ وَهُوَ كَحَيْضٍ فِي أَحْكَامِهِ غَيْرَ عِدَّةٍ وَبُلُوغٍ.

Prayer

The five prayers are obligatory upon every Muslim of legal capacity except for anyone who is menstruating or experiencing postpartum bleeding. Whoever, in denial, abandons it has committed apostasy and is subject to apostasy laws.

كِتَابُ الصَّلاةِ

تَجِبُ الخَمْسُ عَلَى كُلِّ مُسْلِمٍ مُكَلَّفٍ إِلَّا حَائِضاً وَنُفَسَاءَ، وَمَنْ تَرَكَهَا جُحُوداً فَقَدْ ارْتَدَّ، وَجَرَتْ عَلَيْهِ أَحْكَامُ المُرْتَدِّينَ.

Adhān and Iqāmah

The adhān and iqāmah are both communal obligations upon free men; it is recommended for individuals and during travel. They are not valid unless in sequence and continuous, per custom, with an intention by a Muslim male who is sane, discerning, speaking, upright (even if only apparently so), and called after the time enters, except for fajr, which is valid after mid-night. The adhān comprises 15 phrases without tarjīʿ[25]. The iqāmah comprises 11 phrases without doubling. Tarjīʿ is permissible in the adhān, as is doubling the iqāmah.

After the adhān is made, it is impermissible to exit the masjid without an excuse or intent to return. Calling the adhān in the right ear of a newborn and the iqāmah in the left is recommended.

---

[25] To quietly utter the shahādatayn and then repeat them loudly totaling 19 phrases.

فَصْلٌ

الأَذَانُ وَالإِقَامَةُ فَرْضَا كِفَايَةٍ عَلَى الرِّجَالِ الأَحْرَارِ. وَيُسَنَّانِ لِمُنْفَرِدٍ وَسَفَراً، وَلا يَصِحَّانِ إِلَّا مُرَتَّبَيْنِ مُتَوَالِيَيْنِ عُرْفاً، بِنِيَّةٍ مِنْ ذَكَرٍ مُسْلِمٍ عَاقِلٍ مُمَيِّزٍ نَاطِقٍ عَدْلٍ وَلَو ظَاهِراً، بَعْدَ دُخُولِ وَقْتٍ لِغَيْرِ فَجْرٍ وَيَصِحُّ لَهُ بَعْدَ نِصْفِ اللَّيْلِ، وَهُوَ خَمْسَ عَشْرَةَ كَلِمَةً بَلا تَرْجِيعٍ، وَهِيَ إِحْدَى عَشْرَةَ بِلا تَثْنِيَةٍ، وَيُبَاحُ تَرْجِيعُهُ وَتَثْنِيَتُهَا.

وَحَرُمَ خُرُوجٌ مِنْ مَسْجِدٍ بَعْدَهُ بِلَا عُذْرٍ أَوْ نِيَّةِ رُجُوعٍ. وَسُنَّ أَذَانٌ فِي يُمْنَى أُذُنَي مَوْلُودٍ حَيْثُ يُولَدُ، وَإِقَامَةٌ فِي اليُسْرَى.

Prerequisites, Pillars, Obligations, Recommendations

The six prerequisites for the validity of prayer include: purity from a ḥadath; entry of the time; concealment of the ʿawrah[26]; avoidance of impurities; facing the qiblah; and making an intention—its location is the heart, its reality is a resolution to do something, and it is not waived in any situation. Its prerequisites are: Islām, sanity, and discernment. The time to make it is at the onset of worship or just before it.

The 14 pillars of prayer are: standing in an obligatory prayer; takbīrat al-iḥrām[27]; recitation of al-Fātiḥah; bowing; raising from it; straightness; prostration; raising from it; sitting between the two prostrations; tranquility in action i.e. stillness even if briefly; the final tashahhud (the pillar of which is, "O Allāh send Your prayers upon Muhammad," after what is sufficient of the first tashahhud which is, "All greetings are for Allāh, peace upon you, O prophet, and the mercy of Allāh. Peace be upon us and upon Allāh's righteous servants. I bear witness that there is no deity worthy of worship but Allāh and that Muhammad is the messenger of Allāh."); sitting for it and the two salāms[28]; the two salāms; and sequence.

It has eight obligations: takbīr (besides iḥrām); tasmīʿ[29] (for the Imām and individual); taḥmīd[30]; the first tasbīḥah[31] in bowing and prostration; "My Lord forgive me" between the two prostrations (for everyone); the first tashahhud; and its sitting. Its recommendations (both statements and actions) do not invalidate it if they are categorically abandoned.

---

[26] Everything which must be concealed during prayer.

[27] The initial utterance of "Allāhu Akbar".

[28] The phrase, "as-salāmu alaykum wa raḥmatullāh", which is said twice, preferably beginning on the right side.

[29] The phrase, "Allāh listens to whom praise Him."

[30] The phrase, "Our Lord, to You belongs all praise."

[31] The phrase, "Glory to my Lord, The Exalted."

فَصْلٌ

وَشُرُوطُ صِحَّةِ الصَّلَاةِ سِتَّةٌ: طَهَارَةُ الْحَدَثِ، وَدُخُولُ الْوَقْتِ، وَسَتْرُ الْعَوْرَةِ، وَاجْتِنَابُ النَّجَاسَةِ، وَاسْتِقْبَالُ الْقِبْلَةِ، وَالنِّيَّةُ، وَمَحَلُّهَا الْقَلْبُ، وَحَقِيقَتُهَا: الْعَزْمُ عَلَى الشَّيْءِ، وَلَا تَسْقُطُ بِحَالٍ. وَشُرُوطُهَا الْإِسْلَامُ، وَالْعَقْلُ، وَالتَّمْيِيزُ، وَزَمَنُهَا أَوَّلُ الْعِبَادَةِ أَوْ قُبَيْلَهَا بِيَسِيرٍ. وَأَرْكَانُ الصَّلَاةِ أَرْبَعَةَ عَشَرَ: قِيَامٌ فِي فَرْضٍ، وَتَكْبِيرَةُ الْإِحْرَامِ، وَقِرَاءَةُ الْفَاتِحَةِ، وَرُكُوعٌ، وَرَفْعٌ مِنْهُ، وَاعْتِدَالٌ، وَسُجُودٌ، وَرَفْعٌ مِنْهُ، وَجُلُوسٌ بَيْنَ السَّجْدَتَيْنِ، وَطُمَأْنِينَةٌ فِي فِعْلٍ، وَهِيَ السُّكُونُ وَإِنْ قَلَّ، وَتَشَهُّدٌ أَخِيرٌ، وَجُلُوسٌ لَهُ، وَلِلتَّسْلِيمَتَيْنِ وَالرُّكْنُ مِنْهُ: "اللَّهُمَّ صَلِّ عَلَى مُحَمَّدٍ" بَعْدَمَا يُجْزِئُ مِنَ التَّشَهُّدِ الْأَوَّلِ، وَالْمُجْزِئُ مِنْهُ: "التَّحِيَّاتُ لِلَّهِ، سَلَامٌ عَلَيْكَ أَيُّهَا النَّبِيُّ وَرَحْمَةُ اللَّهِ، سَلَامٌ عَلَيْنَا وَعَلَى عِبَادِ اللَّهِ الصَّالِحِينَ، أَشْهَدُ أَنْ لَا إِلَهَ إِلَّا اللَّهُ، وَأَنَّ مُحَمَّداً رَسُولُ اللَّهِ"، وَالتَّسْلِيمَتَانِ، وَالتَّرْتِيبُ.

وَوَاجِبَاتُهَا ثَمَانِيَةٌ: تَكْبِيرٌ لِغَيْرِ الْإِحْرَامِ، وَتَسْمِيعٌ لِإِمَامٍ وَمُنْفَرِدٍ، وَتَحْمِيدٌ، وَتَسْبِيحَةٌ أُولَى فِي رُكُوعٍ وَسُجُودٍ، وَ"رَبِّ اغْفِرْ لِي" بَيْنَ السَّجْدَتَيْنِ لِلْكُلِّ، وَتَشَهُّدٌ أَوَّلٌ، وَجُلُوسٌ لَهُ. وَسُنَنُهَا: أَقْوَالٌ وَأَفْعَالٌ لَا تَبْطُلُ بِتَرْكِ شَيْءٍ مِنْهَا مُطْلَقاً.

It has 11 recommended statements: an opening supplication; seeking refuge; saying "In the name of Allāh"; saying "āmīn"; reciting a chapter (in fajr, Friday, 'Eid, voluntary prayers, and the first two of both maghrib and four-rakʿah prayers); audible recitation of the Imām; the statement "[A praise that] fills the heavens and the earth and what lies between them and whatever else You please" after the taḥmīd (for a non-follower); what exceeds one tasbīḥ; asking forgiveness; supplication in the last tashahhud; and qunūt[32] in witr.

There are 45 recommended actions and manners. It is disliked for anyone praying to turn, close their eyes, or touch pebbles, etc.

32 A supplication made during Witr prayer. See the chapter of Recommended Prayers for details.

فَسُنَنُ الأَقْوالِ إِحْدَى عَشْرَةَ وَهِيَ: اسْتِفْتَاحُ، وَتَعَوُّذُ، وَبَسْمَلَةُ، وَقَولُ: "آمِينَ"، وَقِرَاءَةُ سُورَةٍ فِي فَجْرٍ وَجُمْعَةٍ وَعِيدٍ، وَتَطَوُّعٍ، وَأُولَتَيْ مَغْرِبٍ وَرُبَاعِيَّةٍ، وَجَهْرُ إِمَامٍ بِقِرَاءَةٍ، وَقَولُ غَيْرِ مَأْمُومٍ بَعْدَ التَّحْمِيدِ: "مِلْءَ السَّماءِ، وَمِلْءَ الأَرْضِ، وَمِلْءَ مَا شِئْتَ مِنْ شَيْءٍ بَعْدُ" وَمَا زَادَ عَلَى مَرَّةٍ فِي تَسْبِيحٍ، وَسُؤَالُ المَغْفِرَةِ، وَدُعَاءٌ فِي تَشَهُّدٍ أَخِيرٍ، وَقُنُوتٌ فِي وِتْرٍ.

وَسُنَنُ الأَفْعَالِ مَعَ الهَيْئَاتِ خَمْسٌ وَأَرْبَعُونَ. وَيُكْرَهُ لِلمُصَلِّي الْتِفَاتٌ، وَتَغْمِيضُ عَيْنَيْهِ، وَمَسُّ الحَصَى، وَنَحْوُ ذَلِكَ.

Prostration of Forgetfulness

The prostration of forgetfulness is recommended due to forgetfully making a legislated statement in the wrong place, permitted if a recommended act is abandoned, and obligatory if a bowing, prostration, standing, or sitting is added.

The prayer is invalidated if the obligatory prostration of forgetfulness is intentionally abandoned, the time of which is before the salām. If someone gets up, abandoning or forgetting the tashahhud, they are obliged to return to perform it. Returning is disliked if they have stood completely, and impermissible if they have begun recitation. If they return after beginning recitation, the prayer is invalidated — except for that of someone forgetful or ignorant.

If someone produces a ḥadath, speaks (even if forgetfully), audibly laughs, or clears their throat without need (producing two or more letters), it is invalidated, but not if they sleep and then speak, weep out of reverential fear, or are overcome by coughing, sneezing, or yawning, etc.

Anyone who doubts in a pillar or number of rakʿahs is to act upon certainty i.e. the least amount. Doubt has no effect after its completion.

فَصْلٌ

يُسَنُّ سُجُودُ السَّهْوِ لِلمُصَلِّي إِذَا أَتَى بِقَوْلٍ مَشْرُوْعٍ فِي غَيْرِ مَحَلِّهِ سَهْواً، وَيُبَاحُ إِذَا تَرَكَ مَسْنُوْناً، وَيَجِبُ إِذَا زَادَ رُكُوْعاً أَوْ سُجُوداً أَوْ قِيَاماً أَوْ قُعُوْداً.

وَتَبْطُلُ الصَّلَاةُ بِتَعَمُّدِ تَرْكِ سُجُوْدِ السَّهْوِ الوَاجِبِ الَّذِي مَحَلُّهُ قَبْلَ السَّلَامِ، وَإِنْ نَهَضَ المُصَلِّي عَنْ تَرْكِ تَشَهُّدٍ أَوْ نَاسِياً لَزِمَهُ الرُّجُوعُ لِيَتَشَهَّدَ، وَكُرِهَ إِنْ اسْتَتَمَّ قَائِماً، وَحَرُمَ إِنْ شَرَعَ فِي القِرَاءَةِ، وَبَطَلَتْ بِالرُّجُوعِ بَعْدَ الشُّرُوعِ فِي القِرَاءَةِ صَلَاةُ غَيْرِ نَاسٍ وَجَاهِلٍ.

وَإِنْ أَحْدَثَ أَو تَكَلَّمَ وَلَوْ سَهواً أَوْ قَهْقَهَ أَوْ تَنَحْنَحَ بِلَا حَاجَةٍ فَبَانَ حَرْفَانِ بَطَلَتْ، لَا إِنْ نَامَ فَتَكَلَّمَ أَوْ انْتَحَبَ خَشْيَةً أَوْ غَلَبَهُ سُعَالٌ وعُطَاسٌ أَوْ تَثَاؤُبٌ وَنَحْوُهُ.

وَيَبْنِي عَلَى اليَقِينِ وَهُوَ الأَقَلُّ مَنْ شَكَّ فِي رُكْنٍ أَوْ عَدَدِ رَكَعَاتٍ، وَلَا أَثَرَ لِلشَّكِّ بَعْدَ فَرَاغِهَا.

Recommended Prayers

The most virtuous physical voluntary act after military service and seeking knowledge is voluntary prayer. The most emphasized of which is the eclipse prayer, followed by seeking rain, tarāwīḥ, and then witr (the least of which is one rakʿah and the most is 11). The least complete is three with two salāms; one is permitted when prayed continuously.

Its period is between ʿishāʾ and fajr. Qunūt is preferably made after bowing, saying aloud, "O Allāh, we seek Your help, Your guidance and Your forgiveness, and repent to You. We believe in You, trust in You, and we praise You beneficently. We thank You and do not deny You. O Allāh, You alone do we worship and to You we pray and bow down prostrate. To You we hasten to worship and to serve. Our hope is for Your mercy and we fear Your punishment. Surely, Your inevitable punishment of the disbelievers is at hand."

"O Allāh, guide us with those whom You have guided, and strengthen us with those whom You have given strength. Take us to Your care with those whom You have taken to Your care. Bless us in what You have given. Surely, You command and are not commanded. None whom You have committed to Your care shall be humiliated and none whom You have taken as an enemy shall taste glory. You are Blessed, Our Lord, and Exalted. O Allāh, we seek refuge with Your pleasure from Your anger. We seek refuge in Your forgiveness from Your punishment. We seek refuge in You from You. We cannot count Your praises, You are as You have praised Yourself."

Then prayers are sent upon the Prophet ﷺ. The follower says "āmīn". The individual singularizes the pronoun. The face is then wiped over with both hands, while both in and out of prayer.

There are 10 emphasized routine prayers: two rakʿahs before ẓuhr; two rakʿahs after it; two rakʿahs after maghrib; two rakʿahs after ʿishāʾ; and two rakʿahs before fajr. The most emphasized of them is fajr, followed by maghrib and then the others.

فَصْلٌ

أَفْضَلُ تَطَوُّعِ البَدَنِ بَعْدَ الجِهَادِ وَالعِلْمِ صَلَاةُ التَّطَوُّعِ، وَآكَدُهَا كُسُوفٌ، فَاسْتِسْقَاءٌ، فَتَرَاوِيحُ، فَوِتْرٌ، وَأَقَلُّهُ رَكْعَةٌ، وَأَكْثَرُهُ إِحْدَى عَشْرَةَ، وَأَدْنَى الكَمَالِ ثَلَاثٌ بِسَلَامَيْنِ، وَيَجُوزُ بِوَاحِدٍ سَرْداً.

وَوَقْتُهُ مَا بَيْنَ العِشَاءِ وَالفَجْرِ، وَيَقْنُتُ فِيهِ بَعْدَ الرُّكُوعِ نَدْباً فَيَقُولُ جَهْراً: "اللَّهُمَّ إِنَّا نَسْتَعِينُكَ وَنَسْتَهْدِيكَ وَنَسْتَغْفِرُكَ، وَنَتُوبُ إِلَيْكَ، وَنُؤْمِنُ بِكَ، وَنَتَوَكَّلُ عَلَيْكَ، وَنُثْنِي عَلَيْكَ الخَيْرَ كُلَّهُ، وَنَشْكُرُكَ وَلَا نَكْفُرُكَ، اللَّهُمَّ إِيَّاكَ نَعْبُدُ، وَلَكَ نُصَلِّي وَنَسْجُدُ، وَإِلَيْكَ نَسْعَى وَنَحْفِدُ، نَرْجُو رَحْمَتَكَ وَنَخْشَى عَذَابَكَ، إِنَّ عَذَابَكَ الجِدَّ بِالكُفَّارِ مُلْحِقٌ."

"اللَّهُمَّ اهْدِنَا فِيمَنْ هَدَيْتَ، وَعَافِنَا فِيمَنْ عَافَيْتَ، وَتَوَلَّنَا فِيمَنْ تَوَلَّيْتَ، وَبَارِكْ لَنَا فِيمَا أَعْطَيْتَ، وَقِنَا شَرَّ مَا قَضَيْتَ، إِنَّكَ تَقْضِي وَلَا يُقْضَى عَلَيْكَ، إِنَّهُ لَا يَذِلُّ مَنْ وَالَيْتَ، وَلَا يَعِزُّ مَنْ عَادَيْتَ، تَبَارَكْتَ رَبَّنَا وَتَعَالَيْتَ، اللَّهُمَّ إِنَّا نَعُوذُ بِرِضَاكَ مِنْ سَخَطِكَ، وَبِعَفْوِكَ مِنْ عُقُوبَتِكَ، وَبِكَ مِنْكَ لَا نُحْصِي ثَنَاءً عَلَيْكَ أَنْتَ كَمَا أَثْنَيْتَ عَلَى نَفْسِكَ."

ثُمَّ يُصَلِّي عَلَى النَّبِيِّ ﷺ وَيُؤَمِّنُ مَأْمُومٌ، وَيُفْرِدُ مُنْفَرِدٌ الضَّمِيرَ، ثُمَّ يَمْسَحُ وَجْهَهُ بِيَدَيْهِ هُنَا وَخَارِجَ الصَّلَاةِ.

وَالرَّوَاتِبُ المُؤَكَّدَةُ عَشْرٌ: رَكْعَتَانِ قَبْلَ الظُّهْرِ، وَرَكْعَتَانِ بَعْدَهَا، وَرَكْعَتَانِ بَعْدَ المَغْرِبِ، وَرَكْعَتَانِ بَعْدَ العِشَاءِ، وَرَكْعَتَانِ قَبْلَ الفَجْرِ، وَآكَدُهَا الفَجْرُ، ثُمَّ المَغْرِبُ ثُمَّ سَوَاءٌ.

Tarāwīḥ consists of 20 rakʿahs made in congregation during Ramaḍān. Salām is made for every two rakʿahs with an intention before each set. Its time is between the emphasized routine prayer of ʿishāʾ and witr in the masjid; the beginning of the night is preferred. Subsequently, witr is made in congregation.

وَالتَّرَاوِيْحُ عِشْرُوْنَ رَكْعَةً بِرَمَضَانَ جَمَاعَةً، يُسَلِّمُ مِنْهُ كُلَّ ثِنْتَيْنِ بِنِيَّةٍ أَوَّلَ كُلِّ رَكْعَتَيْنِ، وَوَقْتُهَا بَيْنَ سُنَّةِ عِشَاءٍ وَوِتْرٍ فِي مَسْجِدٍ، وَأَوَّلُ اللَّيلِ أَفْضَلُ، وَيُوْتِرُ بَعْدَهَا فِي جَمَاعَةٍ.

Voluntary Prayers

Ṣalāt al-layl is the most virtuous. The last half of the night is better than the first. Qiyām al-layl[33] is recommended and commenced with two short rakʿahs; its intention is made before sleep. Abundant bowing and prostration are more virtuous than prolonged standing.

Ṣalāt al-ḍuḥā is recommended every other day. It is, at least, two rakʿahs and, at most, eight. Its duration is from the end of the prohibited time until just before the zawāl. Taḥiyyat al-masjid[34], Sunnat al-wuḍūʾ[35], and praying between maghrib and ʿishāʾ prayers, considered a part of qiyām al-layl, are recommended.

Ṣalāt al-istikhārah is recommended, even for something good, which is then done immediately after it. Ṣalāt al-ḥājah[36], for Allāh the Most-High or for a fellow man, is recommended, as is ṣalāt al-tawbah[37]. The prostration of recitation, within a short break, is recommended for the reciter and listener. The prostration of gratitude is recommended when a blessing is renewed or harm is avoided.

---

[33] Ṣalāt al-layl/qiyām al-layl refer to voluntary prayers performed at night.

[34] A two-rakʿah prayer performed before sitting in a masjid.

[35] A two-rakʿah prayer performed upon completion of wuḍūʾ.

[36] A prayer performed when one is in need.

[37] A prayer performed when seeking Allāh's pardon.

فَصْلٌ

وَصلاةُ اللَّيْلِ أَفْضَلُ، وَالنِّصْفُ الأَخِيرُ أَفْضَلُ مِنَ الأَوَّلِ، وَيُسَنُّ قِيَامُ اللَّيْلِ، وَافْتِتَاحُهُ بِرَكْعَتَيْنِ خَفِيفَتَيْنِ، وَنِيَّتُهُ عِنْدَ النومِ، وَكَثْرَةُ الرُّكُوعِ وَالسُّجُودِ أَفْضَلُ مِنْ طُولِ القِيَامِ.

وَتُسَنُّ صَلاةُ الضُّحَى غِبًّا، وَأَقَلُّهَا رَكْعَتَانِ، وَأَكْثَرُهَا ثَمَانٍ، وَوَقْتُهَا مِنْ خُرُوجِ وَقْتِ النَّهْيِ إِلَى قُبَيْلِ الزَّوَالِ. وَتُسَنُّ تَحِيَّةُ المَسْجِدِ، وَسُنَّةُ الوُضُوءِ، وَإِحْيَاءُ مَا بَيْنَ العِشَائَيْنِ، وَهُوَ مِنْ قِيَامِ اللَّيْلِ.

وَتُسَنُّ صَلَاةُ الاِسْتِخَارَةِ وَلَوْ فِي خَيْرٍ، وَيُبَادِرُ بِهِ بَعْدَهَا. وَتُسَنُّ صَلَاةُ الحَاجَةِ إِلَى اللَّهِ تَعَالَى أَوْ إِلَى آدَمِيٍّ. وَتُسَنُّ صَلَاةُ التَّوْبَةِ. وَيُسَنُّ سُجُودُ تِلَاوَةٍ مَعَ قَصْرِ فَصْلٍ لِقَارِئٍ وَمُسْتَمِعٍ. وَيُسَنُّ سُجُودُ شُكْرٍ عِنْدَ تَجَدُّدِ نِعْمَةٍ أَو انْدِفَاعِ نِقْمَةٍ.

Prohibited Times

There are five prohibited times which are: from the start of the second fajr until the sun rises; from ʿaṣr until the sun sets; from its rising until it has risen a spear's height; at its zenith until it falls; and at its setting until it completes. In these times, it is absolutely prohibited to begin a voluntary prayer apart from the following: an obligatory make-up prayer; two rakʿahs for ṭawāf[38]; the recommended prayer of fajr (performed on time); or a funeral prayer after fajr or ʿaṣr.

[38] The procession round the Kaʿbah.

وَأَوْقَاتُ النَّهْيِ خَمْسَةٌ: مِنْ طُلُوعِ فَجْرٍ ثَانٍ إِلَى طُلُوعِ الشَّمْسِ، وَمِنْ صَلَاةِ العَصْرِ إِلَى الغُرُوبِ، وَعِنْدَ طُلُوعِهَا إِلَى ارْتِفَاعِهَا قَدْرَ رُمْحٍ، وَعِنْدَ قِيَامِهَا حَتَّى تَزُولَ، وَعِنْدَ غُرُوبِهَا حَتَى يَتِمَّ، فَيَحْرُمُ فِيهَا ابْتِدَاءُ نَفْلٍ مُطْلَقاً، لَا قَضَاءُ فَرْضٍ، وَفِعْلُ رَكْعَتَي طَوَافٍ، وَسُنَّةُ فَجْرٍ أَدَاءً، وَجَنَازَةٌ بَعْدَ فَجْرٍ وَعَصْرٍ.

Congregational Prayer

Congregational prayer, for the five offered prayers, is obligatory upon capable free men—even while traveling. It is not a prerequisite and thus valid from an individual, whose reward will not diminish with an excuse.

It is convened with two (even with a woman or bondservant, but not a young child for an obligatory prayer), apart from Friday and 'Eid prayers.

It is impermissible to lead prayer in a masjid that has an appointed Imām. It is invalid except with his permission, the absence of his disdain, or his tardiness as the time wanes.

Whoever makes takbīr before the Imām's first taslīm has joined the congregation and whoever catches the bowing has caught the rakʿah.

It is recommended to join the Imām, however found. Whatever is caught with him is its end, and what is made up is its beginning. The following are shouldered by the Imām for the follower: reciting; the prostration of forgetfulness and recitation; having a sutrah; the supplication of qunūt; and the first tashahhud, if preceded by one rakʿah.

It is preferred to begin its actions after the Imām, coinciding with him in them or the salām is disliked. It is impermissible to precede him. Making takbīr al-iḥrām, while coinciding with him, or before he concludes, does not count. Intentionally, without excuse, or forgetfully making salām before him, without repeating it after him, is invalid.

It is preferred for the Imām to lighten it, while maintaining completion; to make the recitation in the first longer than the second; and to wait for anyone coming in, so long as it does not harm the follower(s).

فَصْلٌ

صَلَاةُ الجَمَاعَةِ وَاجِبَةٌ لِلْخَمْسِ المُؤَدَّاةِ عَلَى الرِّجَالِ الأَحْرَارِ القَادِرِينَ وَلَوْ سَفَراً، وَلَيْسَتْ شَرْطاً، فَتَصِحُّ مِنْ مُنْفَرِدٍ وَلَا يَنْقُصُ أَجْرُهُ مَعَ عُذْرٍ.

وَتَنْعَقِدُ بِاثْنَيْنِ فِي غَيْرِ جُمُعَةٍ وَعِيدٍ، وَلَوْ بِأُنْثَى أَوْ عَبْدٍ لَا بِصَبِيٍّ فِي فَرْضٍ. وَحَرُمَ أَنْ يَؤُمَّ بِمَسْجِدٍ لَهُ إِمَامٌ رَاتِبٌ، فَلَا تَصِحُّ إِلَّا مَعَ إِذْنِهِ وَعَدَمِ كَرَاهَتِهِ، أَوْ تَأَخُّرِهِ وَضِيقِ الوَقْتِ.

وَمَنْ كَبَّرَ قَبْلَ تَسْلِيمَةِ الإِمَامِ الأُولَى أَدْرَكَ الجَمَاعَةَ، وَمَنْ أَدْرَكَ الرُّكُوعَ أَدْرَكَ الرَّكْعَةَ. وَسُنَّ دُخُولُهُ مَعَ إِمَامِهِ كَيْفَ أَدْرَكَهُ، وَمَا أَدْرَكَ مَعَهُ آخِرُهَا، وَمَا يَقْضِيهِ أَوَّلُهَا، وَيَتَحَمَّلُ عَنْ مَأْمُومٍ قِرَاءَةً، وَسُجُودَ سَهْوٍ وَتِلَاوَةٍ، وَسُتْرَةً وَدُعَاءَ قُنُوتٍ، وَتَشَهُّداً أَوَّلاً إِذَا سُبِقَ بِرَكْعَةٍ.

وَالأَوْلَى أَنْ يَشْرَعَ فِي أَفْعَالِهَا بَعْدَ إِمَامٍ، فَإِنْ وَافَقَهُ فِيهَا وَفِي سَلَامٍ كُرِهَ، وَإِنْ سَبَقَهُ حَرُمَ، وَإِنْ كَبَّرَ لِإِحْرَامٍ مَعَهُ أَوْ قَبْلَ إِتْمَامِهِ لَمْ تَنْعَقِدْ، وَإِنْ سَلَّمَ قَبْلَهُ عَمْداً بِلَا عُذْرٍ أَوْ سَهْواً وَلَمْ يُعِدْهُ بَعْدَهُ بَطَلَتْ.

وَسُنَّ لِإِمَامٍ التَّخْفِيفُ مَعَ الإِتْمَامِ، وَتَطْوِيلُ قِرَاءَةِ الأُولَى عَنِ الثَّانِيَةِ، وَانْتِظَارُ دَاخِلٍ إِنْ لَمْ يَشُقَّ عَلَى مَأْمُومٍ.

Imāmship

The most entitled to lead the prayer is the best reciter and most knowledgeable. The reciter who does not know the rulings of prayer precedes the illiterate jurist, followed (in subsequent order) by the eldest, the noblest, and the most pious and scrupulous; lots are then drawn.

The home resident and Imām of the masjid (even if a bondservant) are more deserving, except for someone who wields authority over them. A free man is preferred over the fully and partially subjugated, and the partially subjugated is preferred over the fully subjugated. The resident, the seeing, the townsman, anyone with wuḍū', the lender, and the renter are all preferred over their opposites.

Leadership of a sinner is categorically invalid, except for jumuʿah and ʿEid if unable to pray behind another.

It is valid behind the blind, deaf, uncircumcised, a man with severed hands, feet, or nose, and someone who often solecises without changing the meaning. It is not valid behind a mute or disbeliever. There is no leadership for someone unable to meet a prerequisite or pillar (except with those like him), apart from the appointed Imām of a masjid, whose deficiency will likely end. He is to pray seated and those behind him are to sit; it is valid to stand.

Neither a woman nor a hermaphrodite can lead men or hermaphrodites, nor can the discerning lead the mature in an obligatory prayer. There is no imāmship for the following: the deliberately impure or contaminated with najāsah (it is however valid for the follower if both he and the follower were ignorant until its completion); or an illiterate (i.e. someone that cannot properly read al-Fātiḥah, who renders a diphthong what is not to be rendered as such, or who solecises in a way which changes the meaning and is incapable of correcting himself), except for those with a similar condition(s).

فَصْلٌ

الأَولَى بِالإِمَامَةِ الأَجْوَدُ قِرَاءَةً الأَفْقَهُ، وَيُقَدَّمُ قَارِئٌ لَا يَعْلَمُ فِقْهَ صَلَاتِهِ عَلَى فَقِيهٍ أُمِّيٍّ، ثُمَّ الأَسَنُّ، ثُمَّ الأَشْرَفُ، ثُمَّ الأَتْقَى وَالأَوْرَعُ، ثُمَّ يُقْرَعُ،

وَصَاحِبُ البَيْتِ وَإِمَامُ المَسْجِدِ وَلَو عَبْداً أَحَقُّ إِلَّا مِنْ ذِي سُلْطَانٍ فِيهِمَا، وَحُرٌّ أَولَى مِنْ عَبْدٍ وَمُبَعَّضٍ، وَمُبَعَّضٌ أَولَى مِنْ عَبْدٍ، وَحَاضِرٌ، وَبَصِيرٌ، وَحَضَرِيٌّ، وَمُتَوَضِّئٌ، وَمُعِيرٌ، وَمُسْتَأْجِرٌ، أَولَى مِنْ ضِدِّهِم.

وَلَا تَصِحُّ إِمَامَةُ فَاسِقٍ مُطْلَقاً إِلَّا فِي جُمُعَةٍ وَعِيدٍ تَعَذَّراً خَلْفَ غَيْرِهِ.

وَتَصِحُّ خَلْفَ أَعْمَى أَصَمَّ، وَأَقْلَفَ، وَأَقْطَعَ يَدَيْنِ، أَوْ رِجْلَينِ أَوْ أَنفٍ، وَكَثِيرِ لَحْنٍ لَمْ يُحِلْ المَعْنَى، لَا خَلْفَ أَخْرَسَ وَكَافِرٍ، وَلَا إِمَامَةُ عَاجِزٍ عَنْ شَرْطٍ أَوْ رُكْنٍ إِلَّا بِمِثْلِهِ إِلَّا الإِمَامَ الرَّاتِبَ بِمَسْجِدٍ المَرْجُوَّ زَوَالُ عِلَّتِهِ فَيُصَلِّي جَالِساً، وَيَجْلِسُونَ خَلْفَهُ، وَتَصِحُّ قِيَاماً.

وَلَا إِمَامَةُ امْرَأَةٍ وَخُنْثَى لِرِجَالٍ أَوْ خَنَاثَى، وَلَا مُمَيِّزٍ لِبَالِـغٍ فِي فَرْضٍ، وَلَا إِمَامَةُ مُحْدِثٍ أَوْ نَجِسٍ يَعْلَمُ ذَلِكَ، فَإِنْ جَهِلَ هُوَ وَمَأْمُومٌ حَتَّى انْقَضَتْ، صَحَّتْ لِمَأْمُومٍ، وَلَا إِمَامَةُ أُمِّيٍّ—وَهُوَ مَنْ لَا يُحْسِنُ الفَاتِحَةَ أَوْ يُدْغِمُ فِيهَا مَا لَا يُدْغَمُ، أَوْ يَلْحَنُ لَحْناً يُحِيلُ المَعْنَى عَجْزاً عَنْ إِصْلَاحِهِ إِلَّا بِمِثْلِهِ.

To stand in front of the congregation is recommended. Even for iḥrām, the prayer is invalid if performed in front of him (based on the back of the foot). An individual or hermaphrodite is obliged to stand on his right, which is permitted for a woman, though preferred that she stands behind him. The prayer is not valid on his left while his right is vacant or if performed alone[39] for the duration of at least one rakʿah.

If both are in the masjid, following is categorically valid if the Imām's movements are known. If they are not gathered inside, it is stipulated that the Imām, or those behind him, are seen, even if just during a part of it.

It is disliked for the Imām to be elevated a cubit or more above the follower, but not vice versa. Attending a masjid or congregation after eating onion, radish, etc. is disliked until the odor subsides.

---

[39] In a row by themselves.

وَسُنَّ وُقُوفُ جَمَاعَةٍ مُتَقَدِّماً عَلَيْهِمْ، فَإِنْ تَقَدَّمَهُ مَأْمُومٌ وَلَوْ بِإِحْرَامٍ لَمْ تَصِحَّ صَلَاتُهُ، وَالِاعْتِبَارُ بِمُؤَخَّرِ قَدَمٍ، وَيَقِفُ الْوَاحِدُ أَوِ الْخُنْثَى عَنْ يَمِينِهِ وُجُوباً، وَالْمَرْأَةُ خَلْفَهُ نَدْباً، وَيَجُوزُ عَنْ يَمِينِهِ، وَمَنْ صَلَّى عَنْ يَسَارِهِ مَعَ خُلُوِّ يَمِينِهِ، أَوْ رَكْعَةً مُنْفَرِداً لَمْ تَصِحَّ صَلَاتُهُ، وَإِذَا جَمَعَهُمَا مَسْجِدٌ صَحَّتِ الْقُدْوَةُ مُطْلَقاً بِشَرْطِ الْعِلْمِ بِانْتِقَالَاتِ الْإِمَامِ، وَإِنْ لَمْ يَجْمَعْهُمَا شُرِطَ رُؤْيَةُ الْإِمَامِ أَوْ مَنْ وَرَاءَهُ وَلَوْ فِي بَعْضِهَا.

وَكُرِهَ عُلُوُّ إِمَامٍ عَلَى مَأْمُومٍ ذِرَاعاً فَأَكْثَرَ لَا عَكْسُهُ.

وَكُرِهَ حُضُورُ مَسْجِدٍ وَجَمَاعَةٍ لِمَنْ أَكَلَ بَصَلاً أَوْ فُجْلاً وَنَحْوَهُ حَتَّى يَذْهَبَ رِيحُهُ.

Excused from Congregation

The following cases are excused from attending Friday and congregational prayers: when sick or fearful of sickness (while not in the masjid; when holding back either urine or stool; when food is presented while hungry (it is allowed to eat until satiated); when looking for someone lost; whoever fears the loss or destruction of their property or earnings; fears the death of a relative or close friend; fears harm from the authorities, rain, etc.; from the persistence of a debtor while insolvent; or loss of a travel group, etc.

فَصْلٌ

يُعْذَرُ بِتَرْكِ جُمُعَةٍ وَجَمَاعَةٍ مَرِيضٌ، وَخَائِفُ حُدُوثِ مَرَضٍ لَيْسَا بِالمَسْجِدِ، وَمَنْ يُدَافِعُ أَحَدَ الأَخْبَثَيْنِ، وَمَنْ بِحَضْرَةِ طَعَامٍ يَحْتَاجُ إِلَيْهِ، وَلَهُ الشِّبَعُ، أَوْ لَهُ ضَائِعٌ يَرْجُوهُ، أَوْ يَخَافُ ضِيَاعَ مَالِهِ أَوْ ضَرَراً فِيهِ أَوْ فِي مَعِيشَةٍ يَحْتَاجُهَا، أَوْ مَوتَ قَرِيبِهِ أَوْ رَفِيقِهِ، أَوْ ضَرَراً مِنْ سُلْطَانٍ أَوْ مَطَرٍ وَنَحْوِهِ، أَوْ مُلازَمَةَ غَرِيمٍ لَهُ وَلَا شَيْءَ مَعَهُ، أَوْ فَوْتَ رُفْقَةٍ وَنَحْوَ ذَلِكَ.

Prayer of the Ill

It is required that the ill pray while standing (even in the bowing posture), while leaning or resting upon someone employed (if capable of payment). If they are unable to do that, however, sitting is permitted and sitting cross-legged is preferred. If they are unable to do that, then on their side, the right of which is better. If they are unable to do that, they gesture to prostrate and bow to the best of their ability, making the prostration lower. If they are unable to do that, they signal with their eyes while the action is present in their heart; the same applies to the statements of someone unable to speak.

So long as a sound mind is present, prayer is not waived. If standing or sitting becomes possible during the prayer, they must be done and the prayer then completed. If standing is possible, an obligatory prayer performed on a vessel while seated is not valid. It is valid on a standing or advancing mount for the following reasons: being harmed by mud, rain, etc.; fear of being separated from a travel party; fear for one's life from an enemy; or being unable to mount after dismounting. It is a must to face toward the qiblah and do what is possible. The resting place of the limbs is considered during prostration, so unnecessarily putting the forehead on fluffy cotton or praying on a swing invalidates it.

فَصْلٌ

يَلْزَمُ المَرِيْضَ أَنْ يُصَلِّيَ قَائِماً، وَلَوْ كَرَاكِعٍ مُعْتَمِداً أَوْ مُسْتَنِداً بِأُجْرَةٍ يَقْدِرُ عَلَيْهَا، فَإِنْ لَمْ يَسْتَطِعْ فَقَاعِداً مُتَرَبِّعًا نَدْباً، وَكَيْفَ قَعَدَ جَازَ، فَإِنْ لَمْ يَسْتَطِعْ فَعَلَى جَنْبِهِ، وَالأَيْمَنُ أَفْضَلُ، وَيُومِئُ بِرُكُوعٍ وَسُجُودٍ عَاجِزٌ عَنْهُمَا مَا أَمْكَنَهُ، وَيَجْعَلُ السُّجُودَ أَخْفَضَ، فَإِنْ عَجَزَ أَوْمَأَ بِطَرْفِهِ مُسْتَحْضِراً الفِعْلَ بِقَلْبِهِ، وَكَذَا القَوْلُ إِنْ عَجَزَ عَنْهُ بِلِسَانِهِ.

وَلَا تَسْقُطُ مَا دَامَ العَقْلُ ثَابِتاً، فَإِنْ قَدَرَ عَلَى قِيَامٍ أَوْ قُعُودٍ فِي أَثْنَائِهَا انْتَقَلَ إِلَيْهِ وَأَتَمَّهَا.

وَلَا تَصِحُّ مَكْتُوبَةٌ فِي سَفِينَةٍ قَاعِداً لِقَادِرٍ عَلَى قِيَامٍ، تَصِحُّ عَلَى رَاحِلَةٍ وَاقِفَةٍ أَوْ سَائِرَةٍ لِتَأَذٍّ بِوَحْلٍ وَمَطَرٍ وَنَحْوِهِ، أَوْ لِخَوْفِ انْقِطَاعٍ عَنْ رُفْقَةٍ، أَوْ خَوْفٍ عَلَى نَفْسِهِ مِنْ نَحْوِ عَدُوٍّ، أَوْ عَجْزِهِ عَنْ رُكُوبٍ إِنْ نَزَلَ، وَعَلَيْهِ الاسْتِقْبَالُ وَمَا يَقْدِرُ عَلَيْهِ، وَيُعْتَبَرُ المَقَرُّ لِأَعْضَاءِ السُّجُودِ، فَلَو وَضَعَ جَبْهَتَهُ عَلَى قُطْنٍ مَنْفُوشٍ أَوْ صَلَّى فِي أُرْجُوحَةٍ وَلَا ضَرُورَةَ لَمْ تَصِحَّ.

Shortening Prayer

It is recommended to shorten a four-rakʿah prayer for anyone who intends permissible travel (including tourism and sightseeing) to a specific destination which reaches 16 farsakhs[41] (i.e. two days underway by land or sea), if they surpass the homes of their village or tents of their people.

Though shortening is better, completion is not disliked. Repeating is not required of anyone who returns before reaching the distance. Whoever intends unlimited residence in a place, residence for more than four days, or follows a resident, is to complete it. Perpetually shortening is legislated due to being withheld wrongfully, due to rain, or staying to handle a need (without the intention to reside for more than four days),—while not knowing when it will end.

---

41 Approximately 85 US miles; 138 km.

فَصْلٌ

يُسَنُّ قَصْرُ الصَّلَاةِ الرُّبَاعِيَّةِ لِمَن نَوَى سَفَراً مُبَاحاً، وَلَوْ لِنُزْهَةٍ أَوْ فُرْجَةٍ لِمَحَلٍّ مُعَيَّنٍ يَبْلُغُ سِتَّةَ عَشَرَ فَرْسَخاً بَرّاً وَبَحْراً، وَهِيَ يَوْمَانِ قَاصِدَانِ إِذَا فَارَقَ بُيُوتَ قَرْيَتِهِ العَامِرَةِ أَوْ خِيَامَ قَوْمِهِ.

وَلَا يُكْرَهُ إِتْمَامٌ، وَالقَصْرُ أَفْضَلُ، وَلَا يُعِيدُ مَنْ قَصَرَ ثُمَّ رَجَعَ قَبْلَ اسْتِكْمَالِ المُسَافَةِ.

وَمَنْ نَوَى إِقَامَةً مُطْلَقَةً بِمَوْضِعٍ، أَوْ أَكْثَرَ مِنْ أَرْبَعَةِ أَيَّامٍ، أَوْ ائْتَمَّ بِمُقِيمٍ، أَتَمَّ، وَإِنْ حُبِسَ ظُلْماً أَوْ بِمَطَرٍ أَوْ أَقَامَ لِحَاجَةٍ بِلَا نِيَّةِ إِقَامَةٍ فَوْقَ أَرْبَعَةِ أَيَّامٍ، وَلَا يَدْرِي مَتَى تَنْقَضِي، قَصَرَ أَبَداً.

Combining Prayer

It is permitted to combine ẓuhr with ʿaṣr and maghrib with ʿishāʾ in either of their times[42]. It is preferred to avoid it, except for the gatherings of ʿArafah and Muzdalifah, which is then recommended.

Combining can be done in the following eight cases: traveling the distance in which shortening is allowed; the ill who face difficulty if not combined; a wet-nurse due to difficulty from abundant filth; pseudo-menstruation etc.; anyone incapable of purifying themselves or making tayammum for every prayer; not knowing the time, e.g. the blind etc.; or due to some excuse or work which permits abandoning Friday and congregational prayers.

Combining between maghrib and ʿishāʾ is specifically permitted (even if prayed at home) due to snow, cold, ice, mud, strong cold wind, and rain which soaks the clothes, coupled with difficulty.

Regarding advancing or delaying, the best is that which is easiest. If they are equal, then delaying is preferred.

Sequence is an absolute prerequisite for combining. The following are prerequisites for combining during the time of the first prayer: the intention to combine before the iḥrām of the first; not separating the second (except with the equivalent of the iqāmah or a light wuḍūʿ), which would thus be invalided by an emphasized routine prayer between them; the presence of an excuse at the beginning of both and the first salām; its continuity (except when combining for rain etc.) until the completion of the second. Therefore, it is not invalidated if someone makes iḥrām for the first because of rain, which ceases and does not continue though it produces mud. If it does not[43], it is.

---

[42] By combining Ẓuhr and ʿAṣr in either Ẓuhr or ʿAṣr time and combing Maghrib and ʿIshāʾ in either Maghrib or ʿIshāʾ time.

[43] Produce mud.

فَصْلٌ

يُبَاحُ جَمْعٌ بَيْنَ ظُهْرٍ وَعَصْرٍ وَعِشَائَيْنِ بِوَقْتِ إِحْدَاهُمَا، وَتَرْكُهُ أَفْضَلُ غَيْرَ جَمْعَيْ عَرَفَةَ وَمُزْدَلِفَةَ فَيُسَنُّ.

وَيُجْمَعُ فِي ثَمَانِ حَالَاتٍ: بِسَفَرِ قَصْرٍ، وَمَرِيضٌ يَلْحَقُهُ بِتَرْكِهِ مَشَقَّةٌ، وَمُرْضِعٌ لِمَشَقَّةِ كَثْرَةِ نَجَاسَةٍ، وَمُسْتَحَاضَةٌ وَنَحْوُهَا، وَعَاجِزٌ عَنْ طَهَارَةٍ أَوْ تَيَمُّمٍ لِكُلِّ صَلَاةٍ أَوْ عَنْ مَعْرِفَةِ وَقْتٍ كَأَعْمَى وَنَحْوِهِ، أَوْ لِعُذْرٍ أَوْ شُغْلٍ يُبِيحُ تَرْكَ جُمُعَةٍ وَجَمَاعَةٍ.

وَيَخْتَصُّ بِجَوَازِ جَمْعِ العِشَائَيْنِ، وَلَوْ صَلَّى بِبَيْتِهِ، ثَلْجٌ وَبَرَدٌ وَجَلِيدٌ، وَوَحْلٌ وَرِيحٌ شَدِيدَةٌ بَارِدَةٌ، وَمَطَرٌ يَبُلُّ الثِّيَابَ، وَتُوجَدُ مَعَهُ مَشَقَّةٌ.

وَالأَفْضَلُ فِعْلُ الأَرْفَقِ مِنْ تَقْدِيمِ جَمْعٍ أَوْ تَأْخِيرِهِ، فَإِنِ اسْتَوَيَا فَتَأْخِيرٌ أَفْضَلُ.

وَيُشْتَرَطُ لَهُ تَرْتِيبٌ مُطْلَقًا، وَلِجَمْعٍ بِوَقْتِ أُولَى نِيَّةٌ عِنْدَ إِحْرَامِهَا، وَأَنْ لَا يُفَرِّقَ بَيْنَهُمَا إِلَّا بِقَدْرِ إِقَامَةٍ وَوُضُوءٍ خَفِيفٍ، فَيَبْطُلُ بِرَاتِبَةٍ بَيْنَهُمَا، وَوُجُودُ العُذْرِ عِنْدَ افْتِتَاحِهِمَا، وَسَلَامِ الأُولَى، وَاسْتِمْرَارُهُ فِي غَيْرِ جَمْعِ مَطَرٍ وَنَحْوِهِ إِلَى فَرَاغِ الثَّانِيَةِ، فَلَوْ أَحْرَمَ بِالأُولَى لِمَطَرٍ ثُمَّ انْقَطَعَ فَلَمْ يَعُدْ، فَإِنْ حَصَلَ وَحْلٌ لَمْ يَبْطُلْ وَإِلَّا بَطَلَ.

Additionally, if travel concludes with the first prayer, the combining and shortening are invalidated. It is, however, to be completed and is valid as an obligatory prayer. If travel is concluded during the second, they[44] are invalid, but it is to be completed as a voluntary prayer.

The only prerequisites to combine in the second's time are to have the intention from the first's time (so long as there is still time to make it) and the presence of the excuse at the time of the second.

It is not a prerequisite of validity to have only one Imām. It is, therefore, valid if the follower prays: both behind two Imāms; behind someone not combining; one alone and the other in congregation; leading one in the first and another in the second; or with someone not combining.

---

[44] Combining and shortening are impermissible.

وَإِنْ انْقَطَعَ سَفَرٌ بِأُوْلَى بَطَلَ الجَمْعُ وَالقَصْرُ فَيَتِمُّهَا، وَتَصِحُّ فَرْضاً، وَبِثَانِيَةٍ بَطَلَا، وَيَتِمُّهَا نَفْلاً.

وَيُشْتَرَطُ لِجَمْعٍ بِوَقْتِ ثَانِيَةٍ نِيَّتُهُ بِوَقْتِ أُوْلَى مَا لَمْ يَضِقْ عَنْ فِعْلِهَا، وَبَقَاءُ عُذْرٍ إِلَى دُخُولِ وَقْتِ الثَّانِيَةِ لَا غَيْرُ.

وَلَا يُشْتَرَطُ لِصِحَّةٍ اتِّحَادُ إِمَامٍ وَمَأْمُومٍ، فَلَوْ صَلَّاهُمَا خَلْفَ إِمَامَيْنِ، أَوْ خَلْفَ مَنْ لَمْ يَجْمَعْ، أَوْ إِحْدَاهُمَا مُنفَرِداً وَالأُخْرَى جَمَاعَةً أَوْ بِمَأْمُومٍ الأُوْلَى وَبِآخَرِ الثَّانِيَةَ، أَوْ بِمَنْ لَمْ يَجْمَعْ، صَحَّ.

Fear Prayer

Ṣalāt al-khawf (which has six modes) is valid during permissible combat, even as a resident, due to fear of an enemy's attack. If fear becomes severe, prayer is made both on foot and mounted, while facing towards the qiblah or any other direction. Even if possible, it is not required to begin prayer facing towards it. They gesture per their ability. During prayer, it is permitted to strike and move, if needed, which does not invalidate it due to excessive duration.

It is recommended to carry something for defense which is not heavy, e.g. a sword or knife. It is also permitted to carry najas without having to repeat the prayer.

فَصْلٌ

تَصِحُّ صَلَاةُ الخَوفِ بِقِتَالٍ مُبَاحٍ، وَلَوْ حَضراً مَعَ خَوْفِ هَجْمِ العَدُوِّ عَلَى سِتَّةِ أَوْجُهٍ، وَإِذَا اشْتَدَّ الخَوْفُ صَلُّوا رِجَالاً وَرُكْبَاناً لِلْقِبْلَةِ وَغَيْرِهَا وَلَا يَلْزَمُ افْتِتَاحُهَا إِلَيْهَا وَلَوْ أَمْكَنَ يُومِئُونَ طَاقَتَهُمْ وَلِمُصَلٍّ كَرٌّ وَفَرٌّ لِمَصْلَحَةٍ وَلَا تَبْطُلُ بِطُولِهِ.

وَسُنَّ لَهُ فِيهَا حَمْلُ مَا يَدْفَعُ بِهِ عَنْ نَفْسِهِ وَلَا يُثْقِلُهُ كَسَيْفٍ وَسِكِّينٍ، وَجَازَ لِحَاجَةٍ حَمْلُ نَجَسٍ، وَلَا يُعِيدُ.

Friday Prayer

Jumuʿah is obligatory upon the following: free resident Muslim males of legal capacity in an area with buildings (even if constructed of cane); travelers not permitted to shorten prayer; and residents living outside the city an explicit distance of one farsakh[45] or less between them and its location (from the minaret).

It is not obligatory upon the following: those permitted to shorten; the bondsman; partially subjugated; women; and hermaphrodites. It will suffice for whoever attends[46], however it is not convened with them and they, as well as non-residents, are not to be counted as a part of the 40. Likewise, their imāmship for it is not valid.

The following are four prerequisites of its validity, none of which include the ruler's permission:

1. Time—from the beginning of the time for ʿEid to the end of ẓuhr. It is obligated at the zawāl and is preferred after it.

2. The presence of 40 locals including the Imām.

3. Their attendance, even if among them (but not all) are the mute or deaf. If they decrease in number before its completion, they continue as ẓuhr.

4. To begin with two sermons in exchange for two rakʿahs. Their five prerequisites are: time; intention; occurrence during residency; attendance of 40; and delivery by someone whose imāmship is valid.

---

45 5.31 US miles/8.43 km

46 From the above-mentioned categories.

فَصْلٌ

تَجِبُ الجُمُعَةُ عَلَى كُلِّ مُسْلِمٍ مُكَلَّفٍ ذَكَرٍ حُرٍّ مُسْتَوطِنٍ بِبِنَاءٍ وَلَوْ مِنْ قَصَبٍ، وَعَلَى مُسَافِرٍ لَا يُبَاحُ لَهُ القصرُ، وَعلى مُقيمٍ خَارِجَ البَلَدِ إِذَا كَانَ بَيْنَهُ وَبَيْنَ مَوْضِعِهَا مِنَ المَنَارَةِ نَصّاً فَرْسَخٌ فَأَقَلُّ.

وَلَا تَجِبُ عَلَى مَنْ يُبَاحُ لَهُ القَصْرُ وَلَا عَبْدٍ وَلَا مُبَعَّضٍ وَلَا امْرَأَةٍ وَلَا خُنْثَى، وَمَنْ حَضَرَهَا أَجْزَأَتْهُ، وَلَمْ تَنْعَقِدْ بِهِ، فَلَا يُحْسَبُ هُوَ وَلَا مَنْ لَيْسَ مِنْ أَهْلِ البَلَدِ مِنَ الأَرْبَعِينَ، وَلَا تَصِحُّ إِمَامَتُهُمْ فِيهَا.

وَشُرِطَ لِصِحَّتِهَا أَرْبَعَةُ شُرُوطٍ - لَيْسَ مِنْهَا إِذْنُ الإِمَامِ:

أَحَدُهَا: الوَقْتُ، وَهُوَ مِنْ أَوَّلِ وَقْتِ العِيدِ إِلَى آخِرِ وَقْتِ الظُّهْرِ، وَتَلْزَمُ بِزَوَالٍ وَبَعْدَهُ أَفْضَلُ.

الثَّانِي: اسْتِيطَانُ أَرْبَعِينَ وَلَوْ بِالإِمَامِ.

الثَّالِثُ: حُضُورُهُمْ، وَلَوْ كَانَ فِيهِمْ خُرْسٌ أَوْ صُمٌّ لَا كُلُّهُمْ، فَإِنْ نَقَصُوا قَبْلَ إِتْمَامِهَا اسْتَأْنَفُوا ظُهْراً.

الرَّابِعُ: تَقَدُّمُ خُطْبَتَيْنِ بَدَلَ رَكْعَتَيْنِ مِنْ شَرْطِهِمَا خَمْسَةُ أَشْيَاءَ:

الوَقْتُ، وَالنِّيَّةُ، وَوُقُوعُهُمَا حَضَراً، وَحُضُورُ الأَرْبَعِينَ، وَأَنْ يَكُونَ مِمَّنْ تَصِحُّ إِمَامَتُهُ فِيهَا.

They have six pillars which are: praise of Allāh; prayers upon Allāh's messenger ﷺ; recitation of a verse from Allāh's Book; counsel to have taqwa of Allāh; continuity of both sermons with the prayer; and audible delivery so that the required number hears without hindrance.

It is invalidated with unpermitted speech (even if minute) and, if delivered in a language other than Arabic, is like recitation and thus invalid except due to inability. No such exception is made for recitation. The following are recommended: delivery on the minbar or an elevated location; delivery while standing and leaning on a sword or staff; shortening them both (the second being shorter); raising the voice in both, per ability; and supplication for the Muslims. It is permissible to supplicate for someone specific, such as the ruler. It is not blameworthy to deliver the sermon from a paper.

Speaking is prohibited while the Imām is delivering the sermon and is close enough to be heard; it is permitted when he is quiet between them or begins to supplicate.

وَأَرْكَانُهُمَا سِتَّةٌ: حَمْدُ اللهِ، وَالصَّلَاةُ عَلَى رَسُولِ اللهِ ﷺ، وَقِرَاءَةُ آيَةٍ مِنْ كِتَابِ اللهِ، وَالوَصِيَّةُ بِتَقْوَى اللهِ، وَمُوَالَاتُهُمَا مَعَ الصَّلَاةِ، وَالجَهْرُ بِحَيْثُ يُسْمِعُ العَدَدَ المُعْتَبَرَ حَيْثُ لَا مَانِعُ.

وَيُبْطِلُهَا كَلَامٌ مُحَرَّمٌ، وَلَوْ يَسِيراً، وَهِيَ بِغَيْرِ العَرَبِيَّةِ كَقِرَاءَةٍ، فَلَا تَصِحُّ إِلَّا مَعَ العَجْزِ غَيْرَ القِرَاءَةِ.

وَتُسَنُّ عَلَى مِنْبَرٍ أَوْ مَوْضِعٍ عَالٍ، وَأَنْ يَخْطُبَ قَائِماً مُعْتَمِداً عَلَى سَيْفٍ أَوْ عَصَا، وَقَصْرُهُمَا، وَالثَّانِيَةُ أَقْصَرُ، وَرَفْعُ الصَّوْتِ بِهِمَا حَسَبَ الطَّاقَةِ، وَالدُّعَاءُ لِلْمُسْلِمِينَ، وَيُبَاحُ لِمُعَيَّنٍ كَالسُّلْطَانِ، وَلَا بَأْسَ أَنْ يَخْطُبَ مِنْ صَحِيفَةٍ.

وَيَحْرُمُ الكَلَامُ وَالإِمَامُ يَخْطُبُ، وَهُوَ مِنْهُ بِحَيْثُ يَسْمَعُهُ، وَيُبَاحُ إِذَا سَكَتَ بَيْنَهُمَا أَوْ شَرَعَ فِي دُعَاءٍ.

Friday Prayer Location

The Friday prayer is two rakʿahs. Performing it, and ʿEid, in more than one place in the city is impermissible, unless out of necessity (i.e. a lack of space, remoteness, or fear of tribulation, etc.). If the need ceases, the valid prayer is the one attended or permitted by the ruler. If the prayers are equal in their permission or lack thereof, the first to perform iḥrām for the prayer is valid. If how it occurred is unknown, they pray it as ẓuhur.

Reciting sūrat al-Kahf and making abundant supplication and prayers of peace upon the Prophet ﷺ is recommended during the day. Whoever enters while the Imām is delivering the sermon should not sit until they pray two short rakʿahs.

فَصْلٌ

وَالجُمُعَةُ رَكْعَتَانِ، وَحَرُمَ إِقَامَتُهَا وَعِيدٍ فِي أَكْثَرَ مِنْ مَوْضِعٍ مِنَ البَلَدِ إِلَّا لِحَاجَةٍ كَضِيقٍ وَبُعْدٍ وَخَوْفِ فِتْنَةٍ وَنَحْوِهِ، فَإِنْ عُدِمَتْ الحَاجَةُ فَالصَّحِيحَةُ مَا بَاشَرَهُ الإِمَامُ أَوْ أَذِنَ فِيهَا، فَإِنْ اسْتَوَتَا فِي إِذْنٍ أَوْ عَدَمِهِ فَالسَّابِقَةُ بِالإِحْرَامِ هِيَ الصَّحِيحَةُ، وَإِنْ جَهِلَ كَيْفَ وَقَعَتَا صَلُّوا ظُهْراً.

وَسُنَّ قِرَاءَةُ سُورَةِ الكَهْفِ فِي يَوْمِهَا، وَكَثْرَةُ دُعَاءٍ وَصَلَاةٍ عَلَى النَّبِيِّ ﷺ، وَمَنْ دَخَلَ وَالإِمَامُ يَخْطُبُ لَمْ يَجْلِسْ حَتَّى يَرْكَعَ رَكْعَتَيْنِ خَفِيفَتَيْنِ.

'Eid Prayers

The 'Eid prayers are communal obligations. Their times are like that of ṣalāt al-ḍuḥā.

Their prerequisites are like jumuʿah, except for the two sermons. If 'Eid goes unknown until after the zawāl, it is to be made up the following day. It is recommended to pray it in a nearby, per custom, barren area.

It is recommended: for the follower to go walking early, after fajr prayer, in their best dress; for the Imām to delay his attendance until the time of prayer; to spend on the family; to give charity; and to return on a different road other than that of arrival.

It is to be prayed as two rakʿahs before the sermon. Takbīr is made in the first (after the opening supplication but before seeking refuge) six times. In the second, it is made five times before recitation. The hands are raised with every takbīr while saying, "Allāh is ever Greatest. Much praise belongs to Allāh, Glory to Him morning and evening. May the prayer of Allāh and plentiful peace be upon Muhammad and his family." If desired, something else can be said.

There is no dhikr that should be mentioned after the final tabkīr of each of them. Then al-Fātiḥah is recited followed by Sabbiḥ[47] in the first rakʿah, and al-Ghāshiyah in the second. After the salām, two sermons are delivered, the rulings of which are like that of the Friday sermons, including the impermissibility of speaking during the sermon.

It is recommended to begin the first with nine continuous takbīrs and the second with seven, while standing. On the Fiṭr, those in attendance are encouraged to give charity and are told what to distribute. They should be encouraged on Aḍḥā to slaughter a sacrificial animal, as well as taught its rulings. The extra takbīrs, dhikr between them, and the sermons, are recommended.

---

[47] Sūrat al-ʿAlā

فَصْلٌ

وَصلَاةُ العِيدَيْنِ فَرْضُ كِفَايَةٍ، وَوَقْتُهَا كَصَلَاةِ الضُّحَى.

وَشُرُوطُهَا: كَالجُمُعَةِ مَا عَدَا الخُطْبَتَيْنِ، فَإِنْ لَمْ يُعْلَمْ بِالعِيدِ إِلَّا بَعْدَ الزَّوَالِ صَلَّوْا مِنَ الغَدِ قَضَاءً. وَتُسَنُّ بِصَحْرَاءَ قَرِيبَةً عُرْفاً.

وَسُنَّ تَبْكِيرُ مَأْمُومٍ بَعْدَ صَلَاةِ الصُّبْحِ عَلَى أَحْسَنِ هَيْئَةٍ مَاشِياً، وَتَأَخُّرُ إِمَامٍ إِلَى وَقْتِ الصَّلَاةِ، وَالتَّوْسِعَةُ عَلَى الأَهْلِ، وَالصَّدَقَةُ، وَرُجُوعُهُ فِي غَيْرِ طَرِيقِ غُدُوِّهِ.

وَيُصَلِّيهَا رَكْعَتَيْنِ قَبْلَ الخُطْبَةِ، وَيُكَبِّرُ فِي الأُولَى بَعْدَ الاسْتِفْتَاحِ وَقَبْلَ التَّعَوُّذِ سِتّاً، وَفِي الثَّانِيَةِ قَبْلَ القِرَاءَةِ خَمْساً، يَرْفَعُ يَدَيْهِ مَعَ كُلِّ تَكْبِيرَةٍ وَيَقُولُ: "اللهُ أَكْبَرُ كَبِيراً، وَالحَمْدُ لِلهِ كَثِيرًا، وَسُبْحَانَ اللهِ بُكْرَةً وَأَصِيلاً، وَصَلَّى اللهُ عَلَى مُحَمَّدٍ النَّبِيِّ وَآلِهِ وَسَلَّمَ تَسْلِيماً كَثِيراً"، وَإِنْ أَحَبَّ قَالَ غَيْرَ ذَلِكَ.

وَلَا يَأْتِي بِذِكْرٍ بَعْدَ التَّكْبِيرَةِ الآخِرَةِ فِيهِمَا، ثُمَّ يَقْرَأُ الفَاتِحَةَ ثُمَّ سَبِّحْ فِي الرَّكْعَةِ الأُولَى ثُمَّ الغَاشِيَةَ فِي الثَّانِيَةِ، فَإِذَا سَلَّمَ خَطَبَ خُطْبَتَيْنِ، وَأَحْكَامُهُمَا كَخُطْبَتَيِ الجُمُعَةِ حَتَّى فِي تَحْرِيمِ الكَلَامِ حَالَ الخُطْبَةِ.

وَسُنَّ أَنْ يَسْتَفْتِحَ الأُولَى بِتِسْعِ تَكْبِيرَاتٍ نَسَقاً، وَالثَّانِيَةَ بِسَبْعٍ قَائِماً، يَحُثُّهُمْ فِي الفِطْرِ عَلَى الصَّدَقَةِ وَيُبَيِّنُ لَهُمْ مَا يُخْرِجُونَ، وَيُرَغِّبُهُمْ فِي الأَضْحَى فِي الأُضْحِيَةِ، وَيُبَيِّنُ لَهُمْ حُكْمَهَا. وَالتَّكْبِيرَاتُ الزَّوَائِدُ وَالذِّكْرُ بَيْنَهُمَا وَالخُطْبَتَانِ سُنَّةٌ.

Performing voluntary prayers or to making up a missed prayer in its location (before the prayer or after it) just before departing is disliked

If missed, it is recommended to make it up the same day in its prescribed manner.

وَكُرِهَ تَنَفُّلٌ وَقَضَاءُ فَائِتَةٍ قَبْلَ الصَّلَاةِ بِمَوْضِعِهَا وَبَعْدَهَا قُبَيْلَ مُفَارَقَتِهِ.

وَسُنَّ لِمَنْ فَاتَتْهُ قَضَاؤُهَا فِي يَوْمِهَا عَلَى صِفَتِهَا.

Takbīr of ʿEid

Unrestricted takbīr is recommended. It is also recommended to utter it publicly and aloud (for males only[48]) during the night of both ʿEids, while proceeding to attend them, the Fiṭr being more emphasized, until the end of their sermons, and during all 10 days of Dhul-Hijjah. The restricted takbīr proceeds every obligatory prayer performed in congregation, beginning from fajr prayer on the day of ʿArafah until ʿasr on the last day of tashrīq[49]. For the muḥrim[50], it begins from ẓuhr prayer on the day of naḥr. The Imām is to make the takbīr while facing the people.

It is not recommended after the ʿEid prayer. Its manner, uttered in an even number[51], is; "Allāh is the greatest, Allāh is the greatest, there is no deity worthy of worship except Allāh. Allāh is the greatest, Allāh is the greatest, To Allāh belongs all praise."

Saying, "May Allāh accept from both us and you," is not blameworthy, nor is taʿrīf[52] throughout the lands during the evening of ʿArafah.

[48] Females should not utter the takbīr loudly, especially in the presence of men.

[49] The 11th, 12th, and 13th of Dhul-Ḥijjah.

[50] Someone in the state of iḥrām.

[51] The takbir i.e. saying Allāhu Akbar, is uttered twice like the adhān and not once or three times.

[52] To gather in the masjid for remembrance and supplication.

فَصْلٌ

وسَنَّ التَّكْبِيرُ المُطْلَقُ، وَإِظهارُه، وجهرُ غيرِ أُنْثَى بِهِ فِي لَيْلَتَيِ العِيدَيْنِ، وَفِي الخُرُوجِ إِلَيْهِمَا إِلَى فَرَاغِ الخُطْبَةِ فِيهِمَا، وَفِطْرٌ آكَدُ، وَفِي كُلِّ عشْرِ ذِي الحِجَّةِ، وَالتَّكْبِيرُ المُقَيَّدُ عقِبَ كُلِّ فَرِيضَةٍ فِي جَمَاعَةٍ مِنْ صَلَاةِ فَجْرِ يَوْمَ عَرَفَةَ إِلَى عَصْرِ آخِرِ أَيَّامِ التَّشْرِيقِ إِلَّا لِمُحْرِمٍ فَمِنْ صَلَاةِ ظُهْرِ يَوْمَ النَّحْرِ، وَيُكَبِّرُ الإِمَامُ مُسْتَقْبِلَ النَاسِ.

وَلَا يُسَنُّ عَقِبَ صَلَاةِ عِيدٍ فِي صِفَتِهِ شَفْعًا: اللَّهُ أَكْبَرُ، اللَّهُ أَكْبَرُ، لَا إِلَهَ إِلَّا اللَّهُ وَاللَّهُ أَكْبَرُ، اللَّهُ أَكْبَرُ، وَلِلَّهِ الحَمْدُ.

وَلَا بَأْسَ بِقَوْلِهِ لِغَيْرِهِ: تَقَبَّلَ اللَّهُ مِنَّا وَمِنْكَ، وَلَا بِالتَّعْرِيفِ عَشِيَّةَ لَيْلَةِ عَرَفَةَ بِالأَمْصَارِ.

Eclipse Prayer

Ṣalāt al-kusūf is recommended and without a sermon. Its time is from its onset until emergence and is not made up if missed. It consists of two rakʿahs. In each rakʿah there are two standings and two bowings. It is recommended to recite a long chapter and prolong the tasbīḥ, as well as making the first rakʿah longer than the second. It is valid if performed like a voluntary prayer. It is not performed for any other sign (e.g. darkness during the day, light during the night, strong wind, or thunder), except for a continuous earthquake.

فَصْلٌ

صَلَاةُ الكُسُوفِ سُنَّةٌ مِنْ غَيْرِ خُطْبَةٍ، وَوَقْتُهَا مِنْ ابْتِدَائِهِ إِلَى التَّجَلِّي، وَلَا تُقْضَى إِنْ فَاتَتْ، وَهِيَ رَكْعَتَانِ، كُلُّ رَكْعَةٍ بِقِيَامَيْنِ وَرُكُوعَيْنِ. وَسُنَّ تَطْوِيلُ سُورَةٍ وَتَسْبِيحٍ، وَكَوْنُ أُولَى كُلٍّ أَطْوَلُ، وَتَصِحُّ كَالنَّافِلَةِ، وَلَا يُصَلَّى لِآيَةٍ غَيْرِهِ كَظُلْمَةٍ نَهَاراً، وَضِيَاءٍ لَيْلاً، وَرِيحٍ شَدِيدَةٍ، وَصَوَاعِقَ إِلَّا لِزَلْزَلَةٍ دَائِمَةٍ.

Rain Prayer

Ṣalāt al-istisqā' is recommended if the land becomes barren and there is a drought. Its manner and rulings are like 'Eid prayer. It, and the previous prayer, are more virtuous in congregation. If the Imām wishes to go out for it, he is to exhort the people, order them to repent, to abandon oppression, leave quarreling, and to give charity and fast—neither of which are binding by his order. He is to assign them a day on which to assemble and he is to go out humbled, submissive, subservient, obedient, clean but not perfumed, in the company of the religious people of righteousness and maturity.

It is recommended for the discerning children, and is permissible for young children and livestock, to attend. The prayer is performed and then one sermon is delivered. It is commenced with takbīr like the 'Eid sermon. Forgiveness should be sought abundantly and verses that contain an order to do so should be recited.

It is recommended to stand out in the rain when it begins, to make wuḍū' and ghusl with it, and to bring out furnishings and clothing to be rained on. If it becomes fearfully abundant, it is recommended to say, "O Allāh, let it pass us and not fall upon us, but upon the hills and mountains, and the center of the valleys, and upon the forested lands. 'Our Lord, and burden us not with that which we have no ability to bear'" until the end of the verse e.g. al-Baqarah: 286.

It is recommended to say, "Rain has showered us, by the grace and mercy of Allāh."

فَصْلٌ

تُسَنُّ صَلَاةُ الاسْتِسْقَاءِ إِذَا أَجْدَبَتِ الأَرْضُ، وَقَحَطَ المَطَرُ.

وَصِفَتُهَا وَأَحْكَامُهَا كَصَلَاةِ عِيدٍ، وَهِيَ وَالَّتِي قَبْلَهَا جَمَاعَةً أَفْضَلُ، وَإِذَا أَرَادَ الإِمَامُ الخُرُوجَ وَعَظَ النَّاسَ وَأَمَرَهُمْ بِالتَّوْبَةِ وَالخُرُوجِ مِنَ المَظَالِمِ، وَتَرْكِ التَّشَاحُنِ، وَالصَّدَقَةِ وَالصَّوْمِ، وَلَا يَلْزَمَانِ بِأَمْرِهِ، وَيَعِدُهُمْ يَوْماً يَخْرُجُونَ فِيهِ، وَيَخْرُجُ مُتَوَاضِعاً مُتَخَشِّعاً مُتَذَلِّلاً مُتَضَرِّعاً مُتَنَظِّفاً لَا مُتَطَيِّباً، وَمَعَهُ أَهْلُ الدِّينِ وَالصَّلَاحِ وَالشُّيُوخُ.

وَسُنَّ خُرُوجُ صَبِيٍّ مُمَيِّزٍ، وَيُبَاحُ خُرُوجُ أَطْفَالٍ، وَبَهَائِمَ، فَيُصَلِّي ثُمَّ يَخْطُبُ خُطْبَةً وَاحِدَةً يَفْتَتِحُهَا بِالتَّكْبِيرِ كَخُطْبَةِ عِيدٍ، وَيُكْثِرُ فِيهَا الاسْتِغْفَارَ وَقِرَاءَةَ الآيَاتِ الَّتِي فِيهَا الأَمْرُ بِهِ. وَسُنَّ وُقُوفٌ فِي أَوَّلِ المَطَرِ وَتَوَضُّؤٌ وَاغْتِسَالٌ مِنْهُ وَإِخْرَاجُ رَحْلِهِ وَثِيَابِهِ لِيُصِيبَهَا، وَإِنْ كَثُرَ حَتَّى خِيفَ مِنْهُ سُنَّ قَوْلُ: "اللَّهُمَّ حَوَالَيْنَا وَلَا عَلَيْنَا، اللَّهُمَّ عَلَى الظِّرَابِ وَالآكَامِ وَبُطُونِ الأَوْدِيَةِ وَمَنَابِتِ الشَّجَرِ" ﴿رَبَّنَا وَلَا تُحَمِّلْنَا مَا لَا طَاقَةَ لَنَا بِهِ﴾ الآيَةَ [البقرة: 286].

وَسُنَّ قَوْلُ: "مُطِرْنَا بِفَضْلِ اللَّهِ وَرَحْمَتِهِ".

Funerals

It is recommended to prepare for death and remember it often. It is also recommended to visit the sick every other day at the onset of their sickness, in both the day and night, as well as during the nights of Ramaḍān. It is also recommended to remind them to repent and write a will. Visitors should pray for their health and wellbeing and should not sit with them too long. It is a must that they have a good assumption of Allāh.

It is not obligatory to medicate, even if there is perceived benefit. Abandoning it is more virtuous and it is prohibited with the impermissible. It is permissible to write some Qur'ānic verses and dhikr and place them in a vessel and have the pregnant (due to labor difficulties) and the ill drink it. If it descends upon them, it is recommended for the gentlest of their family to quench their thirst with water or a drink, moisten their lips with cotton, to implicitly direct them to say, "There is no deity worthy of worship except Allāh" once (and no more than three times) if they speak, they are gently urged to repeat it, and to recite al-Fātiḥah.

It is recommended at its time to turn them toward the qiblah on their right side, provided space is available; otherwise on their back with their soles facing the qiblah. They are to rely upon Allāh regarding those they love and bequeath to those they believe to be most deserving. If they die, it is recommended to close their eyes, which is permissible to be done by a maḥram[53] male or female. It is disliked for menstruating women or anyone in a major state of ritual impurity to do it, or to come near them.

It is also recommended: to say, "In the name of Allāh, upon the passing of Allāh's messenger"; to fasten the jaws closed; to soften the joints; to remove the clothes; to cover them with cloth; to be hasty in preparing them if they did not die suddenly; and to divide the will and settle their debt.

---

[53] Anyone permanently impermissible to marry.

كِتَابُ الجَنَائِزِ

يُسَنُّ الاسْتِعْدَادُ لِلْمَوْتِ، وَالإِكْثَارُ مِنْ ذِكْرِهِ.

وَتُسَنُّ عِيَادَةُ مَرِيضٍ مُسْلِمٍ غِبًّا مِنْ أَوَّلِ المَرَضِ بُكْرَةً وَعَشِيَّةً، وَفِي رَمَضَانَ لَيْلاً، وَتَذْكِيرُهُ التَّوْبَةَ وَالوَصِيَّةَ، وَيَدْعُو لَهُ عَائِدٌ بِالعَافِيَةِ وَالصَّلَاحِ، وَلَا يَطِيلُ الجُلُوسَ عِنْدَهُ، وَيَنْبَغِي أَنْ يُحْسِنَ ظَنَّهُ بِاللَّهِ،

وَلَا يَجِبُ التَّدَاوِي، وَلَوْ ظَنَّ نَفْعَهُ، وَتَرْكُهُ أَفْضَلُ، وَيَحْرُمُ بِمُحَرَّمٍ، وَيُبَاحُ كَتْبُ قُرْآنٍ وَذِكْرٍ بِإِنَاءٍ لِحَامِلٍ لِعُسْرِ الوِلَادَةِ، وَمَرِيضٍ وَيُسْقِيَانِهِ، وَإِذَا نَزَلَ بِهِ سُنَّ لِأَرْفَقِ أَهْلِهِ بِهِ تَعَاهُدُ بَلِّ حَلْقِهِ بِمَاءٍ أَوْ شَرَابٍ، وَتَنْدِيَةُ شَفَتَيْهِ بِقُطْنَةٍ، وَتَلْقِينُهُ: لَا إِلَهَ إِلَّا اللَّهُ " مَرَّةً وَلَمْ يَزِدْ عَلَى ثَلَاثٍ إِلَّا أَنْ يَتَكَلَّمَ فَيُعِيدُهُ بِرِفْقٍ، وَقِرَاءَةُ الفَاتِحَةِ.

وَيُسَنُّ عِنْدَهُ تَوْجِيهُهُ إِلَى القِبْلَةِ عَلَى جَنْبِهِ الأَيْمَنِ مَعَ سَعَةِ المَكَانِ وَإِلَّا فَعَلَى ظَهْرِهِ وَأَخْمَصَاهُ إِلَى القِبْلَةِ، وَيَعْتَمِدُ عَلَى اللَّهِ فِيمَنْ يُحِبُّ، وَيُوصِي لِلأَرْجَحِ فِي نَظَرِهِ، فَإِذَا مَاتَ سُنَّ تَغْمِيضُ عَيْنَيْهِ، وَيُبَاحُ مِنْ مَحْرَمٍ ذَكَرٍ أَوْ أُنْثَى، وَيُكْرَهُ مِنْ حَائِضٍ وَجُنُبٍ، وَأَنْ يَقْرَبَاهُ.

وَقَوْلُ: "بِسْمِ اللَّهِ وَعَلَى وَفَاةِ رَسُولِ اللَّهِ ﷺ"، وَشَدُّ لَحْيَيْهِ بِعِصَابَةٍ، وَتَلْيِينُ مَفَاصِلِهِ، وَخَلْعُ ثِيَابِهِ، وَسَتْرُهُ بِثَوْبٍ، وَإِسْرَاعُ تَجْهِيزِهِ إِنْ مَاتَ غَيْرَ فَجْأَةٍ، وَتَفْرِقَةُ وَصِيَّتِهِ، وَيَجِبُ فِي قَضَاءِ دَيْنِهِ.

Washing

Washing the deceased is a communal obligation, except for the martyred in battle and wrongly killed (even if they both be female or not of legal capacity). It is a prerequisite that the water be ṭahūr and permissible. It is a prerequisite that the washer be Muslim, sane, and of discerning age; it is preferred they be trustworthy and know the rulings of washing. When washing begins, their ʿawrah is to be concealed from view under a covering.

The attendance of anyone else, besides an assistant, is disliked. An intention is made and Allāh's name is mentioned, which is an obligation just like the washing of someone alive. It is recommended to raise the head (of someone not pregnant) close to the sitting position and lightly press their stomach[55]. Incense should be burned, and abundant water should be poured. The washer should then wrap their hand in a moist cloth and clean the deceased. It is impermissible to touch the ʿawrah of someone seven years old. The pointer finger and thumb (both wrapped in cloth moistened with water) are placed between their lips to clean their teeth as well as inside their nostrils to clean them both. It is recommended that wuḍū' be performed for them (without putting water in their mouth or nose). Then their head is washed with the foam of the sidr[56] and their body with its sediment. The right side of the body should be washed first and then the left. Water is then poured over their entire body.

Washing them only once if nothing comes out is disliked. It is obligatory to repeat it up to seven times if something does come out. If something comes out after that, they are to be stuffed with cotton. If that does not hold, pure dirt is used. The area is washed and then it is obligatory to make wuḍū' for them. The miscarriage of four months is treated like a live newborn.

---

[55] To express any immediate contents.

[56] Ziziphus Lotus; the leaves of which are ground and mixed in water to produce foam.

فَصْلٌ

وَغَسْلُهُ فَرْضُ كِفَايَةٍ سِوَى شَهِيدِ مَعْرَكَةٍ، وَمَقْتُولٍ ظُلْماً، وَلَوْ كَانَا أُنْثَيَيْنِ أَوْ غَيْرَ مُكَلَّفَيْنِ. وَشُرِطَ فِي مَاءٍ طَهُورِيَّةٌ وَإِبَاحَةٌ، وَفِي غَاسِلٍ إِسْلَامٌ، وَعَقْلٌ، وَتَمْيِيزٌ، وَالأَفْضَلُ ثِقَةٌ عَارِفٌ بِأَحْكَامِ الغُسْلِ. وَإِذَا أَخَذَ فِي غَسْلِهِ سَتَرَ عَوْرَتَهُ عَنْ العُيُونِ تَحْتَ سِتْرٍ.

وَكُرِهَ حُضُورُ غَيْرِ مُعِينٍ فِي غَسْلِهِ، ثُمَّ نَوَى وَسَمَّى وُجُوباً كَغَسْلِ الحَيِّ. وَسُنَّ أَنْ يَرْفَعَ رَأْسَ غَيْرِ حَامِلٍ إِلَى قُرْبِ جُلُوسِهِ، وَيَعْصِرَ بَطْنَهُ بِرِفْقٍ، وَيَكُونَ ثَمَّ بَخُورٌ، وَيُكْثِرَ صَبَّ المَاءِ حِينَئِذٍ ثُمَّ يَلُفُّ عَلَى يَدِهِ خِرْقَةً مَبْلُولَةً فَيُنَجِّيهِ بِهَا. وَحَرُمَ مَسُّ عَوْرَةِ مَنْ لَهُ سَبْعُ سِنِينَ، ثُمَّ يُدْخِلُ إِبْهَامَهُ وَسَبَّابَتَهُ وَعَلَيْهِمَا خِرْقَةٌ مَبْلُولَةٌ بِمَاءٍ بَيْنَ شَفَتَيْهِ فَيَمْسَحُ أَسْنَانَهُ، وَفِي مَنْخِرَيْهِ فَيُنَظِّفُهُمَا، ثُمَّ يُوَضِّئُهُ اسْتِحْبَاباً، وَلَا يُدْخِلُ مَاءً فِي فَمِهِ وَأَنْفِهِ، وَيَغْسِلُ رَأْسَهُ بِرَغْوَةِ السِّدْرِ وَبَدَنَهُ بِثُفْلِهِ، وَيَغْسِلُ شِقَّهُ الأَيْمَنَ ثُمَّ الأَيْسَرَ، ثُمَّ يُفِيضُ المَاءَ عَلَى جَمِيعِ بَدَنِهِ.

وَكُرِهَ اقْتِصَارٌ عَلَى غَسْلِهِ مَرَّةً إِنْ لَمْ يَخْرُجْ شَيْءٌ، فَإِنْ خَرَجَ وَجَبَ إِعَادَتُهُ إِلَى سَبْعٍ، فَإِنْ خَرَجَ بَعْدَهَا حُشِيَ بِقُطْنٍ، فَإِنْ لَمْ يَسْتَمْسِكْ فَبِطِينٍ حُرٍّ، ثُمَّ يَغْسِلُ المَحَلَّ وَيُوَضَّأُ وُجُوباً. وَسَقْطُ الأَرْبَعَةِ أَشْهُرٍ كَمَوْلُودٍ حَيّاً.

Shrouding

Their shrouding is a communal obligation. It is an obligatory right of Allāh and a right of the deceased, comprised of one garment which does not show the skin and completely covers them.

It is recommended to shroud a man with three white cotton shrouds; anymore is disliked. After being fumed with fragrance e.g. oud[58], they are laid on top of each other. The finest of them is fixed as the outside layer with ḥanūṭ[59] between each. They are then laid down on top of them. The left side of the inner-most shroud is brought to their right side and then the right is brought to the left. The second and then the third are fashioned in a similar manner. Most of the excess is to be gathered at the head and then they are tied, to be later untied in the grave.

Five garments are recommended for women and hermaphrodites including an izār; khimār; qamīṣ[60]; and two shrouds. For young girls, a qamīṣ and two shrouds are recommended. For boys, one garment is recommended; three are permissible unless their inheritors are not of legal capacity.

---

[58] A fragrance derived from the dark aromatic resin of Agarwood.

[59] A mixture of perfumes prepared specifically for the deceased which may include camphor, sandalwood, and calamus.

[60] The izār (a skirt-like garment which covers from the waist down) is worn first, followed by the qamīṣ (a floor-length gown with long sleeves) is worn next, followed by a khimār (a veil which covers the head and is wrapped around under the chin).

فَصْلٌ

وَتَكْفِينُهُ فَرْضُ كِفَايَةٍ، وَيَجِبُ لِحَقِّ اللهِ تَعَالَى وَلِحَقِّهِ ثَوْبٌ وَاحِدٌ لَا يَصِفُ الْبَشَرَةَ يَسْتُرُ جَمِيعَهُ.

وَسُنَّ تَكْفِينُ رَجُلٍ فِي ثَلَاثِ لَفَائِفَ بِيضٍ مِنْ قُطْنٍ، وَكُرِهَ فِي أَكْثَرَ، تُبْسَطُ عَلَى بَعْضِهَا بَعْدَ تَبْخِيرِهَا بِنَحْوِ عُودٍ، وَتُجْعَلُ الظَّاهِرَةُ أَحْسَنَهَا وَالْحَنُوطُ فِيمَا بَيْنَهَا، ثُمَّ يُوضَعُ عَلَيْهَا مُسْتَلْقِياً ثُمَّ يُرَدُّ طَرَفُ اللِّفَافَةِ الْعُلْيَا مِنَ الْجَانِبِ الْأَيْسَرِ عَلَى شِقِّهِ الْأَيْمَنِ، ثُمَّ الْأَيْمَنُ عَلَى الْأَيْسَرِ، ثُمَّ الثَّانِيَةُ عَلَى الثَّالِثَةِ كَذَلِكَ، وَيُجْعَلُ أَكْثَرُ الْفَاضِلِ عِنْدَ رَأْسِهِ، ثُمَّ يَعْقِدُهَا وَتُحَلُّ فِي الْقَبْرِ. وَسُنَّ لِامْرَأَةٍ وَخُنْثَى خَمْسَةُ أَثْوَابٍ: إِزَارٌ وَخِمَارٌ وَقَمِيصٌ وَلِفَافَتَانِ، وَلِصَغِيرَةٍ قَمِيصٌ وَلِفَافَتَانِ، وَلِصَبِيٍّ ثَوْبٌ وَاحِدٌ، وَيُبَاحُ فِي ثَلَاثَةِ مَا لَمْ يَرِثْهُ غَيْرُ مُكَلَّفٍ.

Funeral Prayer

Praying over the deceased is a communal obligation which is forgone with one person of legal capacity, even if they be a female or bondservant. Offering it in congregation is recommended.

It has eight prerequisites which are: intention; legal capacity; facing the qiblah; covering the ʿawrah; being free of najāsah; the presence of the deceased (if they are in the country); both the one praying and being prayed upon being Muslim; and their purification, even if with earth.

It has seven pillars which are: standing for the obligatory prayer; the four takbīrs; recitation of al-Fātiḥah; praying upon the Prophet ﷺ; supplication for the deceased; the salām; and sequence.

It is recommended for the Imām and the lone individual to stand at the chest of a man and the middle of a woman.

Its description is as follows: make an intention then make takbīr and read al-Fātiḥah; make takbīr and pray upon the Prophet ﷺ (as found in the tashahhud); make takbīr and supplicate for the deceased, which is more virtuous if done with something reported; make takbīr and briefly pause; and then make taslīm (one time is sufficient), even if, "and the mercy of Allāh," is not said.

فَصْلٌ

وَالصَّلَاةُ عَلَيْهِ فَرْضُ كِفَايَةٍ، وَتَسْقُطُ بِمُكَلَّفٍ، وَلَوْ أُنْثَى أَوْ عَبْداً، وَتُسَنُّ جَمَاعَةً.

وَشُرُوطُهَا ثَمَانِيَةٌ: النِّيَّةُ، وَالتَّكْلِيفُ، وَاسْتِقْبَالُ القِبْلَةِ، وَسَتْرُ العَوْرَةِ، وَاجْتِنَابُ النَّجَاسَةِ، وَحُضُورُ المَيِّتِ إِنْ كَانَ بِالبَلَدِ، وَإِسْلَامُ المُصَلِّي وَالمُصَلَّى عَلَيْهِ، وَطَهَارَتُهُمَا وَلَوْ بِتُرَابٍ.

وَأَرْكَانُهَا سَبْعَةٌ: القِيَامُ فِي فَرْضِهَا، وَالتَّكْبِيرَاتُ الأَرْبَعُ، وَقِرَاءَةُ الفَاتِحَةِ، وَالصَّلَاةُ عَلَى النَّبِيِّ ﷺ، وَالدُّعَاءُ لِلْمَيِّتِ، وَالسَّلَامُ، وَالتَّرْتِيبُ.

وَسُنَّ قِيَامُ إِمَامٍ وَمُنْفَرِدٍ عِنْدَ صَدْرِ رَجُلٍ وَوَسَطِ امْرَأَةٍ.

وَصِفَتُهَا: أَنْ يَنْوِيَ ثُمَّ يُكَبِّرَ، وَيَقْرَأَ الفَاتِحَةَ، ثُمَّ يُكَبِّرَ، وَيُصَلِّيَ عَلَى النَّبِيِّ ﷺ كَفِي التَّشَهُّدِ، ثُمَّ يُكَبِّرَ، وَيَدْعُوَ لِلْمَيِّتِ، وَالأَفْضَلُ بِشَيْءٍ مِمَّا وَرَدَ، ثُمَّ يُكَبِّرَ، وَيَقِفَ قَلِيلاً وَيُسَلِّمَ، وَتُجْزِئُ وَاحِدَةٌ، وَلَوْ لَمْ يَقُلْ: وَرَحْمَةُ اللهِ.

Burial

Transporting, burying, and shrouding the deceased are communal obligations; if fulfilled by a non-believer they are no longer required. It is recommended: to walk in front of the funeral procession and ride behind it; to stay close to it; to move quickly; and to make the grave both deep and wide. The following are disliked: raising the voice during it, even if for some dhikr or Qur'ān; placing wood inside the grave or something which is burned by fire; plastering it; or building, writing, walking, or sitting on it.

It is obligatory that the deceased be faced towards the qiblah, recommended to be placed on the right side, and impermissible to bury two or more in one grave without necessity.

The following are recommended: placing the deceased in from the foot-end if feasible (if not, then from anywhere); whoever is placing them to say, "In the name of Allāh, upon the religion of Allāh's messenger ﷺ"; pouring earth over the deceased three times and then heaping it on; implicitly directing the deceased to say the shahādah; supplicating for them after the burial; sprinkling the grave with water; and raising it the height of a hand-span.

It is impermissible to perform a caesarean on a deceased pregnant woman. However, women[61] should extract whom they believe to be alive. If they are unable, she is not to be buried until it dies. If a portion of it comes out while alive, a caesarean is performed for the remainder. If it dies before a caesarean is performed, it is still extracted (sans-caesarean) to be washed and shrouded. If extraction is not possible, whatever has exited is washed and prayed over with her. If it is less than four months, she alone is prayed over.

---

[61] Female medical staff, midwives, etc.

فَصْلٌ

وَحَمْلُهُ وَدَفْنُهُ فَرْضُ كِفَايَةٍ، وَيَسْقُطَانِ، وَتَكْفِينٌ بِكَافِرٍ.

وَسُنَّ كَوْنُ مَاشٍ أَمَامَ الجَنَازَةِ، وَرَاكِبٍ خَلْفَهَا، وَقُرْبٌ مِنْهَا، وَإِسْرَاعٌ بِهَا، وَتَعْمِيقُ قَبْرٍ وَتَوْسِيعُهُ. وَكُرِهَ رَفْعُ الصَّوتِ مَعَهَا وَلَوْ بِذِكْرٍ، وَالقُرْآنِ، وَإِدْخَالُ القَبْرِ خَشَباً أَوْ مَا مَسَّتْهُ النَّارُ، وَتَجْصِيصُهُ، وَبِنَاءٌ، وَكِتَابَةٌ، وَمَشْيٌ، وَجُلُوسٌ عَلَيْهِ.

وَيَجِبُ أَنْ يُسْتَقْبَلَ بِهِ القِبْلَةَ. وَيُسَنُّ عَلَى جَنْبِهِ الأَيْمَنِ، وَحَرُمَ دَفْنُ اثْنَيْنِ فَأَكْثَرَ فِي قَبْرٍ إِلَّا لِضَرُورَةٍ.

وَسُنَّ أَنْ يُدْخَلَ مَيِّتٌ مِنْ عِنْدِ رِجْلَيْهِ إِنْ كَانَ أَسْهَلَ، وَإِلَّا فَمِنْ حَيْثُ سَهُلَ، وَقَوْلُ مُدْخِلٍ: "بِسْمِ اللَّهِ وَعَلَى مِلَّةِ رَسُولِ اللَّهِ ﷺ"، وَحَثْوُ التُّرَابِ عَلَيْهِ ثَلَاثاً ثُمَّ يُهَالُ، وَتَلْقِينُهُ، وَالدُّعَاءُ لَهُ بَعْدَ الدَّفْنِ، وَرَشُّ القَبْرِ بِمَاءٍ، وَرَفْعُهُ قَدْرَ شِبْرٍ.

وَإِنْ مَاتَتْ حَامِلٌ حَرُمَ شَقُّ بَطْنِهَا، وَأَخْرَجَ النِّسَاءُ مَنْ تُرْجَى حَيَاتُهُ، فَإِنْ تَعَذَّرَ لَمْ تُدْفَنْ حَتَّى يَمُوتَ، وَإِنْ خَرَجَ بَعْضُهُ حَيّاً شُقَّ البَاقِي، فَلَوْ مَاتَ قَبْلَ الشَّقِّ أُخْرِجَ حَتَّى يُغْسَلَ، وَيُكَفَّنُ بِلَا شَقٍّ؛ فَإِنْ تَعَذَّرَ إِخْرَاجُهُ غُسِلَ مَا خَرَجَ مِنْهُ وَصُلِّيَ عَلَيْهِ مَعَهَا، وَإِنْ لَمْ يَكُنْ لَهُ أَرْبَعَةُ أَشْهُرٍ فَأَكْثَرُ صُلِّيَ عَلَيْهَا دُونَهُ.

Condolences

It is recommended to give condolences to a Muslim, even if young, within three days. A Muslim grieved by a Muslim is told, "May Allāh magnify your reward, and make your bereavement perfect, and forgive your deceased." Whoever receives condolences responds by saying, "May Allāh answer your supplication and have mercy upon both us and you." Any act of piety done to give the reward to a Muslim, either living or dead, will be of benefit to them.

It is recommended for men to visit the graves, but disliked for women, and impermissible for them if they know something impermissible will happen.

It is permissible to cry for the deceased but nadb[63], niyāḥah[64], tearing the clothes, and striking the cheeks, etc. are impermissible.

The deceased are aware of their visitors on Friday before the sun rises[65].

---

[63] Tearfully lamenting with certain statements.

[64] Wailing replete with lamentation or mentioning the good qualities of the deceased.

[65] Imam Aḥmad mentioned that they always know their visitors, though this time is more stressed.

فَصْلٌ

وَتَعْزِيَةُ مُسْلِمٍ، وَلَوْ صَغِيراً إِلَى ثَلَاثَةِ أَيَّامٍ سُنَّةٌ، فَيُقَالُ لِمُسْلِمٍ مُصَابُ بِمُسْلِمٍ: "أَعْظَمَ اللّٰهُ أَجْرَكَ وَأَحْسَنَ عَزَاكَ، وَغَفَرَ لِمَيِّتِكَ"، وَيَرُدُّ مُعَزًّى بِقَوْلِ: "اِسْتَجَابَ اللّٰهُ دُعَاكَ وَرَحِمَنَا وَإِيَّاكَ."

وَأَيُّ قُرْبَةٍ فُعِلَتْ وَجُعِلَ ثَوَابُهَا لِمُسْلِمٍ حَيٍّ أَوْ مَيِّتٍ نَفَعَهُ ذَلِكَ.

وَتُسَنُّ زِيَارَةُ الْقُبُورِ لِلرِّجَالِ، وَتُكْرَهُ لِلنِّسَاءِ، وَإِنْ عَلِمْنَ أَنَّهُ يَقَعُ مِنْهُنَّ مُحَرَّمٌ حَرُمَتْ.

وَيَجُوزُ الْبُكَاءُ عَلَى الْمَيِّتِ، وَيَحْرُمُ نَدْبٌ، وَنِيَاحَةٌ، وَشَقُّ ثَوْبٍ، وَلَطْمُ خَدٍّ وَنَحْوُهُ.

وَيَعْرِفُ الْمَيِّتُ زَائِرَهُ يَوْمَ الْجُمُعَةِ قَبْلَ طُلُوعِ الشَّمْسِ.

Zakāt[66]

Its obligatory nature has five perquisites which are: Islām; freedom (but not completely and thus obligatory upon the partially subjugated per the degree of their ownership); possessing the niṣāb[67]; full ownership; and completion of one lunar year. It is obligatory upon the wealth of both the young and insane.

It is applied to the following five things: livestock; earthly yields; honey; money; and merchandise.

Its obligation is forgone with the presence of a debt, which diminishes the niṣāb. Whoever dies, while owing zakāt, will have it taken from their estate.

The following are prerequisites for livestock: that they be for milking, breeding, or pasturing (not for labor); that they graze in permissible fields for most of the year; and that they reach the niṣāb.

The lowest niṣāb for camels is five, for which one sheep is due. For 10, there are two. For 15, there are three and for 20, there are four. For 25, there is a one-year-old she-camel. For 36, there is a two-year-old she-camel. For 46, there is a three-year-old she-camel. For 76, there are two two-year-old she-camels. For 91, there are two three-year-old she-camels. For 121, there are three two-year-old she-camels. Then for every 40 thereafter, there is one two-year-old she-camel and for every 50, there is one three-year-old she-camel.

---

[66] It is the right of specific wealth for specific people at a specific time.

[67] The minimum amount of wealth (coupled with certain conditions) liable for zakāt.

كِتَابُ الزَّكَاةِ

شُرُوطُ وُجُوبِهَا خَمْسَةُ أَشْيَاءَ: الإِسْلَامُ، وَالحُرِّيَّةُ لَا كَمَالُهَا، فَتَجِبُ عَلَى مُبَعَّضٍ بِقَدرِ مُلْكِهِ، وَمُلْكُ النِّصَابِ، وَالمُلْكُ التَّامُّ، وَتَمَامُ الحَوْلِ. وَتَجِبُ فِي مَالِ الصَّغِيرِ وَالمَجْنُونِ.

وَهِيَ فِي خَمْسَةِ أَشْيَاءَ: سَائِمَةُ بَهِيمَةِ الأَنْعَامِ، وَالخَارِجُ مِنْ الأَرْضِ، وَالعَسَلُ، وَالأَثْمَانُ، وَعُرُوضُ التِّجَارَةِ.

وَيَمْنَعُ وُجُوبَهَا دَيْنٌ يَنْقُصُ النِّصَابَ، وَمَنْ مَاتَ وَعَلَيْهِ زَكَاةٌ أُخِذَتْ مِنْ تَرِكَتِهِ.

وَشُرِطَ فِي بَهِيمَةِ الأَنْعَامِ أَنْ تُتَّخَذَ لِلدَّرِّ وَالنَّسْلِ وَالتَّسْمِينِ، لَا لِلْعَمَلِ، وَأَنْ تُرْعَى المُبَاحَ أَكْثَرَ الحَوْلِ، وَأَنْ تَبْلُغَ نِصَاباً.

فَأَقَلُّ نِصَابِ الإِبِلِ خَمْسٌ وَفِيهَا شَاةٌ، وَفِي عَشْرٍ شَاتَانِ، وَفِي خَمْسَةَ عَشَرَ ثَلَاثُ شِيَاهٍ، وَفِي عِشْرِينَ أَرْبَعُ شِيَاهٍ، وَفِي خَمْسٍ وَعِشْرِينَ بِنْتُ مَخَاضٍ، وَهِيَ الَّتِي لَهَا سَنَةٌ، وَفِي سِتٍّ وَثَلَاثِينَ بِنْتُ لَبُونٍ، وَهِيَ الَّتِي لَهَا سَنَتَانِ، وَفِي سِتٍّ وَأَرْبَعِينَ حِقَّةٌ، وَهِيَ الَّتِي لَهَا ثَلَاثُ سِنِينَ، وَفِي سِتٍّ وَسَبْعِينَ بِنْتَا لَبُونٍ، وَفِي إِحْدَى وَتِسْعِينَ حِقَّتَانِ، وَفِي مِائَةٍ وَإِحْدَى وَعِشْرِينَ ثَلَاثُ بَنَاتِ لَبُونٍ، ثُمَّ فِي كُلِّ أَرْبَعِينَ بِنْتُ لَبُونٍ، وَفِي كُلِّ خَمْسِينَ حِقَّةٌ.

Cattle & Sheep

The minimum niṣāb for cattle is 30, for which there is a one-year-old bull. For 40, there is a two-year-old cow. For 60, there are two one-year-old bulls. For every 30 thereafter, there is a one-year-old bull and for every 40, there is a two-year-old cow.

The minimum niṣāb for goats/sheep is 40, for which there is either a one-year-old kid or a six-month-old lamb. For 121, there are two. For 201, there are three. For 400, there are four and for every 100 thereafter, there is one.

Combining of two properties based on its terms, renders them as one.

فَصْلٌ

وَأَقَلُّ نِصَابِ البَقَرِ ثَلاثُونَ، وَفِيهَا تَبِيعٌ وَهُوَ مَا لَهُ سَنَةٌ، وَفِي أَرْبَعِينَ مُسِنَّةٌ وَهِيَ الَّتِي لَهَا سَنَتَانِ، وَفِي سِتِّينَ تَبِيعَانِ، ثُمَّ فِي كُلِّ ثَلَاثِينَ تَبِيعٌ، وَفِي كُلِّ أَرْبَعِينَ مُسِنَّةٌ. وَأَقَلُّ نِصَابِ الغَنَمِ أَرْبَعُونَ، وَفِيهَا شَاةٌ مِنَ المَعْزِ لَهَا سَنَةٌ وَاحِدَةٌ أَوْ جَذَعَةٌ مِنَ الضَّأْنِ لَهَا سِتَّةُ أَشْهُرٍ، وَفِي مِائَةٍ وَإِحْدَى وَعِشْرِينَ شَاتَانِ، وَفِي مِائَتَيْنِ وَوَاحِدَةٍ ثَلَاثُ شِيَاهٍ، وَفِي أَرْبَعِمِائَةٍ أَرْبَعُ شِيَاهٍ، ثُمَّ فِي كُلِّ مِائَةِ شَاةٍ شَاةٌ.

وَالخُلْطَةُ بِشَرْطِهَا تُصَيِّرُ المَالَيْنِ كَالمَالِ الوَاحِدِ.

Earthly Yield

Zakāt is obligatory upon every measured and stored item such as grains, staple foods, etc. It is obligatory on all grains like wheat, oats, rice, garbanzo beans, sweet peas, lentils, lupines and ervils, along with cotton, flax, basil and cucumber seeds but not for the likes of nutmeg, figs, grapes, or any other fruits like apples, ambarella, pears, etc. with two prerequisites.

The first is to possess the niṣāb, which is five wasqs after filtering the grains and drying the produce[68].

One wasq[69] equals 60 ṣā'ṣ[70]. One ṣā' equals five and one-third Iraqian pounds[71] which is equivalent to 342 and six-sevenths Damascan pounds[72].

The second is possession at the time of liability, i.e. when grains harden and produce ripens. It is not determined until they are placed on the threshing floor, etc.

One-tenth is obligatory for what has been effortlessly irrigated, one-half of that for what was irrigated with effort, and three-quarters of it for what was irrigated with a combination of the two[73]. If they are equal, consideration is given to the method which yielded the greatest benefit and growth; if it is unknown, one-tenth is due.

Both the one-tenth and land tax are combined for taxable land, i.e. that which has been forcibly conquered and has not been divided among those who are due spoils (besides Makkah) like Egypt, the Levant, and Iraq.

---

[68] Approximate dry measure of 145 L.

[69] One wasq is equivalent to 122.2 kg (270 US lb.).

[70] One ṣā' is equivalent to 2036 g (4.5 US lb.).

[71] One Iraqian pound is equivalent to 381.8 g.

[72] One Damascan pound is equivalent to 5.93 g.

[73] Respectively, 10%, 5%, and 7.5%

فَصْلٌ

تَجِبُ الزَّكَاةُ فِي كُلِّ مَكِيلٍ مُدَّخَرٍ مِنْ حَبَّةٍ مِنْ قُوتِ البَلَدِ وَغَيْرِهِ.

فَتَجِبُ فِي كُلِّ الحُبُوبِ كَالحِنْطَةِ، وَالشَّعِيرِ، وَالأُرُزِّ، وَالحِمَّصِ، وَالجُلُبَّانَ، وَالعَدَسِ، وَالتُّرْمُسِ، وَالكِرْسَنَةِ، وَبِزْرِ القُطْنِ وَالكَتَّانِ، وَبِزْرِ الرَّيَاحِينَ والقِثَّاءِ، لَا فِي نَحْوِ جَوْزٍ وَتِينٍ وَعُنَّابٍ، وَلَا فِي بَقِيَّةِ الفَوَاكِهِ كَتُفَّاحٍ وَإِجَّاصٍ وكُمَّثْرَى وَنحْوِ ذَلِكَ، بِشَرْطَيْنِ:

أَحَدُهُمَا: أَنْ يَبْلُغَ نِصَاباً وَقَدْرُه -بَعْدَ تَصْفِيَةِ حَبٍّ وَجَفَافِ ثَمَرٍ- خَمْسَةُ أَوْسُقٍ، وَالوَسْقُ سِتُّونَ صَاعاً، وَالصَّاعُ خَمْسَةُ أَرْطَالٍ وَثُلُثٌ بِالعِرَاقِيِّ، وَهِيَ ثَلَاثُمِائَةٍ وَاثْنَانِ وَأَرْبَعُونَ رِطْلاً وَسِتَّةُ أَسْبَاعِ رِطْلٍ بِالدِّمَشْقِيِّ.

الثَّانِي: مُلْكُهُ وَقْتَ وُجُوبِهَا، وَهُوَ فِي الحَبِّ اشْتِدَادُهُ، وَفِي الثَّمَرِ بُدُوُّ صَلَاحِهِ، وَلَا يَسْتَقِرُّ إِلَّا فِي جَعْلِهَا فِي بَيْدَرٍ وَنَحْوِهِ.

ويَجِبُ العُشُرُ فِيمَا سُقِيَ بِلَا كُلْفَةٍ، وَنِصْفُهُ فِيمَا سُقِيَ بِهَا، وَثَلَاثَةُ أَرْبَاعِهِ فِيمَا سُقِيَ بِهِمَا، فَإِنْ تَفَاوَتَا اعْتُبِرَ الأَكْثَرُ نَفْعاً وَنُمُوّاً، وَمَعَ الجَهْلِ العُشُرُ.

وَيَجْتَمِعُ عُشْرٌ وَخَرَاجٌ فِي أَرْضٍ خَرَاجِيَّةٍ، وَهِيَ مَا فُتِحَتْ عَنْوَةً، وَلَمْ تُقَسَّمْ بَيْنَ الغَانِمِينَ غَيْرَ مَكَّةَ كَمِصْرٍ وَالشَّامِ وَالعِرَاقِ.

One-tenth of honey is due, regardless if it was taken from uncultivated or owned land. Its niṣāb is 160 Iraqian pounds[75].

Whoever extracts the niṣāb of minerals (after smelting and purification) is obliged to give two and one-half percent immediately. One-fifth of rikāz i.e. buried treasure, even if scant, is due and is to be treated like fay'[76]. Its obligatory payment is not voided by a debt and the remainder belongs to its finder (even if they are an employee), so long as they are not hired to search for it.

---

75 Approximately 61.08 kilograms (135 US pounds).

76 War booty acquired without military action.

وَفِي العَسَلِ العُشْرُ سَوَاءٌ أَخَذَهُ مِنْ مَوَاتٍ أَوْ مَمْلُوكَةٍ، وَنِصَابُهُ مِائَةٌ وَسِتُّونَ رِطْلاً عِرَاقِيَّةً. وَمَنْ اسْتَخْرَجَ مِنْ مَعْدِنٍ نِصَاباً بَعْدَ سَبْكٍ وَتَصْفِيَةٍ فَفِيهِ رُبْعُ العُشْرِ فِي الحَالِ، وَفِي الرِّكَازِ وَهُوَ الكَنْزُ وَلَوْ قَلِيلاً الخُمُسُ، يُصْرَفُ مَصْرِفَ الفَيْءِ، وَلَا يَمْنَعُ مِنْ وُجُوبِهِ دَيْنٌ، وَبَاقِيهِ لِوَاجِدِهِ وَلَوْ أَجِيراً لَا لِطَالِبِهِ.

Gold & Silver

Two and one-half percent of gold and silver must be paid if they reach the niṣāb i.e. 20 mithqāls[77] for gold and 200 dirhams for silver[78]. They can be combined to complete the niṣāb. The value of merchandise can also be combined to one, or both, as well.

There is no zakāt due on permissible jewelry intended for usage or lending (even for whom it is impermissible) so long as they are not trying to avoid payment. It is obligatory on [jewelry] that is impermissible, has been allocated to rent, or has been prepared for expenditure if it reaches the niṣāb.

It is impermissible to adorn the masjid and miḥrāb[79], as well as to plate the roof or walls, with gold or silver. It is obligatory to remove it and pay its zakāt, unless it is worn away and none of it can be collected.

It is permissible for a male to have a silver ring, which is best worn on the left pinky finger. It can be made from more than a mithqāl (so long as it is not customarily excessive), as can a sword's pommel, belt's décor, armor, and helmet; not stirrups, reins, or an inkwell etc.

It is permissible to have a golden sword's pommel and whatever else is necessary. It is permitted for women to have whatever is customary to wear, even if it exceeds 1000 mithqāls. It is also allowed for men and women to wear jewelry made from the likes of gems and jewels.

For-profit sales merchandise is appraised at what would be more advantageous to the poor; either gold or silver.

---

[77] Approximately 85 g.

[78] Approximately 594 g.

[79] A structure at the front of the masjid which indicates the direction of the qiblah.

فَصْلٌ

وَيَجِبُ فِي الذَّهَبِ وَالفِضَّةِ رُبْعُ العُشْرِ إِذَا بَلَغَا نِصَاباً، فَنِصَابُ ذَهَبٍ عِشْرُونَ مِثْقَالاً، وَفِضَّةٍ مِائَتَا دِرْهَمٍ، وَيُضَمُّ أَحَدُهُمَا إِلَى الآخَرِ فِي تَكْمِيلِ النِّصَابِ، وَتُضَمُّ قِيمَةُ عَرْضِ تِجَارَةٍ إِلَى أَحَدِ ذَلِكَ، وَإِلَى جَمِيعِهِ.

وَلَا زَكَاةَ فِي حُلِيٍّ مُبَاحٍ مُعَدٍّ لِلاسْتِعْمَالِ أَوْ إِعَارَةٍ، وَلَوْ لِمَنْ يَحْرُمُ عَلَيْهِ، غَيْرَ فَارٍّ مِنْ زَكَاةٍ.

وَتَجِبُ فِي مُحَرَّمٍ، وَمُعَدٍّ لِلْكِرْيِ أَوْ النَّفَقَةِ إِذَا بَلَغَ نِصَاباً.

وَيَحْرُمُ أَنْ يُحَلَّى مَسْجِدٌ أَوْ مِحْرَابٌ أَوْ يُمَوَّهَ سَقْفٌ أَوْ حَائِطٌ بِنَقْدٍ، وَتَجِبُ إِزَالَتُهُ وَزَكَاتُهُ إِلَّا إِذَا اسْتُهْلِكَ وَلَمْ يَجْتَمِعْ مِنْهُ شَيْءٌ فِيهِمَا.

يُبَاحُ لِذَكَرٍ مِنْ فِضَّةٍ خَاتَمٌ، وَلُبْسُهُ بِخِنْصَرِ يَسَارٍ أَفْضَلُ، وَلَا بَأْسَ بِجَعْلِهِ أَكْثَرَ مِنْ مِثْقَالٍ مَا لَمْ يَخْرُجْ عَنِ العَادَةِ، وَقَبِيعَةُ سَيْفٍ، وَحِلْيَةُ مِنْطَقَةٍ، وَجَوْشَنٌ، وَخُوذَةٌ، لَا رِكَابٌ وَلِجَامٌ وَدَوَاةٌ وَنَحْوُ ذَلِكَ.

وَيُبَاحُ مِنْ ذَهَبٍ قَبِيعَةُ سَيْفٍ، وَمَا دَعَتْ إِلَيْهِ ضَرُورَةٌ، وَلِنِسَاءٍ مَا جَرَتْ عَادَتُهُنَّ بِلُبْسِهِ وَلَوْ زَادَ عَلَى أَلْفِ مِثْقَالٍ، وَلِلرَّجُلِ وَالمَرْأَةِ التَّحَلِّي بِنَحْوِ جَوْهَرٍ وَيَاقُوتٍ.

وَيُقَوَّمُ عَرْضُ التِّجَارَةِ، وَهُوَ مَا يُعَدُّ لِلْبَيْعِ وَالشِّرَاءِ لِأَجْلِ الرِّبْحِ بِالأَحَظِّ لِلْفُقَرَاءِ مِنْ ذَهَبٍ وَفِضَّةٍ.

Fiṭr

Zakāt al-Fiṭr is an obligatory charity at the commencement of Ramaḍān's Fiṭr[80]. It is a designated obligation, distributed like zakāt, and its obligatory nature is not forgone due to a debt unless it is demanded. It is obligatory upon every Muslim to pay for themselves and on behalf of every Muslim under their care (so long as it is in addition to their obligatory spending of both the night and day of ʿEid, what is required of living quarters, servants, transports, books of knowledge needed to read and master, and daily clothing, etc.). If there is not enough for everyone, he should begin with himself then his wife, his bondservant, his mother, his father, his child and then those closest related in inheritance. It is recommended to give it on behalf of a fetus.

It becomes obligatory at sunset on the night of ʿEid al-Fiṭr, is permissible before it by two days, preferable on the same day before the prayer, disliked for the remainder of the day, impermissible to delay after it, and is obligatory to make up. It consists of one ṣāʿ of wheat, barley, dates, raisins, or dried yogurt. The best is dates, then raisins, then wheat, and then the most beneficial. If those are unavailable, any storable grain will suffice. It is permissible for a group to give their Fiṭr to an individual and vice versa.

---

[80] ʿEid al-Fiṭr

فَصْلٌ

وَزَكَاةُ الفِطْرِ صَدَقَةٌ وَاجِبَةٌ بِالفِطْرِ مِنْ رَمَضَانَ، وَتُسَمَّى فَرْضاً، وَمَصْرَفُهَا كَزَكَاةٍ، وَلَا يَمْنَعُ وُجُوبَهَا دَيْنٌ إِلَّا مَعَ طَلَبٍ. وَتَجِبُ عَلَى كُلِّ مُسْلِمٍ إِذَا كَانَتْ فَاضِلَةً عَنْ نَفَقَةٍ وَاجِبَةٍ يَوْمَ العِيدِ وَلَيْلَتَهُ، وَمَا يَحْتَاجُهُ مِنْ مَسْكَنٍ وَخَادِمٍ وَدَابَّةٍ، وَكُتُبِ عِلْمٍ يَحْتَاجُهَا لِنَظَرٍ وَحِفْظٍ، وَثِيَابِ بِذْلَةٍ وَنَحْوِهِ، فَيُخْرِجُ عَنْ نَفْسِهِ، وَعَنْ مُسْلِمٍ يَمُونُهُ، فَإِنْ لَمْ يَجِدْ لِجَمِيعِهِمْ بَدَأَ بِنَفْسِهِ فَزَوْجَتِهِ فَرَقِيقِهِ، فَأُمِّهِ فَأَبِيهِ، فَوَلَدِهِ فَأَقْرَبَ فِي المِيرَاثِ. وَتُسَنُّ عَنْ جَنِينٍ.

وَتَجِبُ بِغُرُوبِ شَمْسِ لَيْلَةِ عِيدِ الفِطْرِ، وَتَجُوزُ قَبْلَهُ بِيَوْمَيْنِ فَقَطْ، وَيَوْمَهُ قَبْلَ الصَّلَاةِ أَفْضَلُ، وَتُكْرَهُ فِي بَاقِيهِ، وَيَحْرُمُ تَأْخِيرُهَا عَنْهُ، وَتُقْضَى وُجُوباً، وَهِيَ صَاعٌ مِنْ بُرٍّ أَوْ شَعِيرٍ أَوْ تَمْرٍ أَوْ زَبِيبٍ أَوْ أَقِطٍ، وَالأَفْضَلُ تَمْرٌ فَزَبِيبٌ فَبُرٌّ فَأَنْفَعُ، فَإِنْ عُدِمَتْ أَجْزَأَ كُلُّ حَبٍّ يُقْتَاتُ، وَيَجُوزُ أَنْ تُعْطِيَ الجَمَاعَةُ فِطْرَتَهُمْ لِوَاحِدٍ وَعَكْسُهُ.

Distribution

It is obligatory to distribute zakāt immediately, if possible, just like an oath or an expiation. It is, however, possible to delay it due to an excuse. Whoever knowingly denies it, even if they distribute it, has committed apostasy. Whoever withholds it, due to stinginess or negligence, will have it taken and whoever knows the impermissibility of such will be penalized. The guardian of the young and mentally ill is required to distribute it on their behalf; the prerequisite of which is the presence of an intention, just like for his own wealth. It is recommended to publicize it and impermissible, but will suffice, to deliver it beyond the distance of shortening in the presence of its recipients. If the one upon whom zakāt is obligatory is in one land and their wealth is in another, it should be distributed in the land in which it is; their fiṭr, and that of those who are a financial responsibility, is to be distributed in their land. It is permissible to prepay it for no more than two years if the niṣāb is met and not from it for the two years[81].

It is only payed to eight categories which are: the poor; the impoverished; those working for the zakāt fund; to soften the hearts; manumission of bondservants; the debtor; in the way of Allāh; and the wayfarer.

It is permissible to limit it to one of the categories and recommended to give it to relatives who are not a financial responsibility. It is permissible for the eligible to ask for it.

It is obligatory to accept lawful wealth given without asking for or desiring it. If someone capable of earning a livelihood becomes solely dedicated to seeking Islamic knowledge (not mere worship) and is unable to balance both their livelihood and studies, they are to be given what they need of zakat, even if that knowledge is not required of them.

---

[81] It is not permitted to prepay zakāt if the payment detracts from the niṣāb.

فَصْلٌ

يَجِبُ إِخْرَاجُ الزَّكَاةِ فَوْراً كَنَذْرٍ وَكَفَّارَةٍ إِنْ أَمْكَنَ، وَلَهُ تَأْخِيرٌ لِعُذْرٍ، وَمَنْ جَحَدَ وُجُوبَهَا عَالِماً كَفَرَ وَلَوْ أَخْرَجَهَا، وَمَنْ مَنَعَهَا بُخْلاً أَوْ تَهَاوُناً أُخِذَتْ مِنْهُ وَعُزِّرَ مَنْ عَلِمَ تَحْرِيمَ ذَلِكَ، وَيَلْزَمُ أَنْ يُخْرِجَ عَنْ الصَّغِيرِ وَالمجْنُونِ وَلِيُّهُمَا، وَشُرِطَ لَهُ نِيَّةُ كَمَالِهِ، وَسُنَّ إِظْهَارُ، وَحَرُمَ نَقْلُهَا إِلَى مَسَافَةِ قَصْرٍ إِنْ وُجِدَ أَهْلُهَا وَتُجْزِئُ، وَإِنْ كَانَ المزَكِّيُّ فِي بَلَدٍ وَمَالُهُ فِي آخَرٍ أَخْرَجَ زَكَاةَ المَالِ فِي بَلَدِ المَالِ، وَأَخْرَجَ فِطْرَتَهُ وَفِطْرَةَ مَنْ لَزِمَتْهُ فِي بَلَدِ نَفْسِهِ، وَيَجُوزُ تَعْجِيلُهَا لِحَوْلَيْنِ فَقَطْ إِذَا كَمُلَ النِّصَابُ لَا مِنْهُ لِلحَوْلَيْنِ.

وَلَا تُدْفَعُ إِلَّا إِلَى الأَصْنَافِ الثَّمَانِيَةِ وَهُمْ: الفُقَرَاءُ، وَالمَسَاكِينُ، وَالعَامِلُونَ عَلَيْهَا، وَالمُؤَلَّفَةُ قُلُوبُهُمْ، وَفِي الرِّقَابِ، وَالغَارِمُونَ، وَفِي سَبِيلِ اللَّهِ، وَابْنِ السَّبِيلِ.

وَيَجُوزُ الاقْتِصَارُ عَلَى وَاحِدٍ مِنْ صِنْفٍ، وَتُسَنُّ إِلَى مَنْ لَا تَلْزَمُهُ مُؤْنَتُهُ مِنْ أَقَارِبِهِ، وَمَنْ أُبِيحَ لَهُ أَخْذُ شَيْءٍ أُبِيحَ لَهُ سُؤَالُهُ.

وَيَجِبُ قَبُولُ مَالٍ طَيِّبٍ أَتَى بِلَا مَسْأَلَةٍ وَلَا اسْتِشْرَافِ نَفْسٍ، وَإِنْ تَفَرَّغَ قَادِرٌ عَلَى التَّكَسُّبِ لِلْعِلْمِ الشَّرْعِيِّ لَا لِلْعِبَادَةِ وَتَعَذَّرَ الجَمْعُ بَيْنَ التَّكَسُّبِ وَالاشْتِغَالِ بِالعِلْمِ أُعْطِيَ مِنْ زَكَاةٍ لِحَاجَتِهِ، وَإِنْ لَمْ يَكُنْ العِلْمُ لَازِماً لَهُ.

Charity

It is not sufficient to distribute it to the following: a non-believer (other than seeking to soften their heart); a bondservant (other than one working independently or buying freedom); both the poor and impoverished who find sufficiency in obligatory spending; and banī Hāshim, i.e. his progeny ﷺ, or their freed bondservants.

If it is unknowingly distributed to other than the deserving, and such a condition is later known, it will not suffice except for someone wealthy assumed to be poor.

Voluntary charity is always recommended. It is better if done secretly; in goodwill; while healthy; in Ramaḍān; in a time of need; during every virtuous time; in every virtuous place; and given to a neighbor or relative - especially while feuding, which is then considered charity and joining the ties of kinship. To make a reminder of charity is a major sin, which nullifies its reward.

فَصْلٌ

وَلَا يُجْزِئُ دَفْعُهَا إِلَى كَافِرٍ غَيْرِ مُؤَلَّفٍ، وَلَا إِلَى كَامِلِ رِقٍّ غَيْرِ عَامِلٍ وَمُكَاتَبٍ، وَلَا إِلَى فَقِيرٍ وَمِسْكِينٍ مُسْتَغْنِيَيْنِ بِنَفَقَةٍ وَاجِبَةٍ، وَلَا لِبَنِي هَاشِمٍ وَهُمْ سُلَالَتُهُ، ﷺ، وَلَا مَوَالِيهِمْ، وَإِنْ دَفَعَهَا لِغَيْرِ مُسْتَحِقِّهَا لِجَهْلٍ ثُمَّ عَلِمَ حَالَهُ لَمْ تُجْزِئْهُ إِلَّا لِغَنِيٍّ ظَنَّهُ فَقِيراً.

وَتُسَنُّ صَدَقَةُ التَّطَوُّعِ كُلَّ وَقْتٍ، وَكَوْنُهَا سِرّاً بِطِيبِ نَفْسٍ فِي صِحَّةٍ، وَرَمَضَانَ، وَوَقْتِ حَاجَةٍ، وَفِي كُلِّ زَمَانٍ وَمَكَانٍ فَاضِلٍ، وَعَلَى جَارٍ وَذَوِي رَحِمٍ لَا سِيَّمَا مَعَ عَدَاوَةٍ، وَهِيَ صَدَقَةٌ وَصِلَةٌ أَفْضَلُ، وَالمَنُّ بِالصَّدَقَةِ كَبِيرَةٌ وَيَبْطُلُ الثَّوَابُ بِهِ.

Fasting

It is to intentionally refrain from specific things during a specific time.

The fast of Ramaḍān[82] becomes obligatory with the sighting of the crescent moon. If it is not sighted in the clear night sky on the 30th of Shaʿbān[83], fasting is not commenced. If, however, its place of rising is obstructed by clouds, dust, etc., it is obligatory to fast with the intention of Ramaḍān as an assumed precautionary ruling, which will suffice if it becomes apparent. The rulings of fasting, tarāwīḥ, and the obligatory expiation for intercourse during it, etc. all apply, so long as it has not been proven to be a day of Shaʿbān. The remaining rulings, such as divorce and manumission of bondservants, do not apply. The crescent, which is visible during the day, is for the following night.

If its sighting is confirmed in one area, everyone else is required to fast. If it is confirmed in the day, it must be fasted and then made up. It, alone, is accepted by one who is of legal capacity and upright; even if by a bondservant or a woman or given without the wording of testimony. It is not restricted to the ruler, and all the remaining rulings apply. Whoever sights it for Shawwāl[84] alone, is not to break the fast, but if they sight it alone for Ramaḍān, and their testimony is rejected, they are required to fast. All the rulings of the month, including divorce, and manumission of bondservants, etc., apply.

---

[82] The ninth month of the Hijra calendar.

[83] The eighth month of the Hijra calendar.

[84] The tenth month of the Hijra calendar.

كِتَابُ الصِّيَامِ

وَهُوَ إِمْسَاكٌ بِنِيَّةٍ عَنْ أَشْيَاءَ مَخْصُوصَةٍ فِي زَمَنٍ مَخْصُوصٍ.

وَصَومُ رَمَضَانَ يَجِبُ بِرُؤْيَةِ هِلَالِهِ، فَإِنْ لَمْ يُرَ مَعَ صَحْوٍ لَيْلَةَ الثَّلَاثِينَ مِنْ شَعْبَانَ لَمْ يَصُومُوا، وَإِنْ حَالَ دُونَ مَطْلَعِهِ غَيْمٌ أَوْ قَتَرٌ أَوْ غَيْرُهُمَا وَجَبَ صِيَامُهُ حُكْماً ظَنِّيًّا احْتِيَاطاً بِنِيَّةِ رَمَضَانَ، وَيُجْزِئُ إِنْ ظَهَرَ مِنْهُ. وَتُثْبَتُ أَحْكَامُ الصَّوْمِ مِنْ صَلَاةِ تَرَاوِيحَ، وَوُجُوبِ كَفَّارَةٍ بِوَطْءٍ فِيهِ وَنَحْوِهِ مَا لَمْ يَتَحَقَّقْ أَنَّهُ مِنْ شَعْبَانَ، وَلَا تُثْبَتُ بَقِيَّةُ الأَحْكَامِ مِنْ نَحْوِ طَلَاقٍ وَعِتَاقٍ، وَالهِلَالُ المَرْئِيُّ نَهَاراً لِلَّيْلَةِ المُقْبِلَةِ.

وَإِذَا ثَبَتَتْ رُؤْيَتُهُ بِبَلَدٍ لَزِمَ الصَّوْمُ جَمِيعَ النَّاسِ، وَإِنْ ثَبَتَتْ نَهَاراً أَمْسَكُوا وَقَضَوْا، وَيُقْبَلُ فِيهِ وَحْدَهُ خَبَرُ مُكَلَّفٍ عَدْلٍ، وَلَوْ عَبْداً أَوْ أُنْثَى أَوْ بِدُونِ لَفْظِ الشَّهَادَةِ، وَلَا يَخْتَصُّ بِحَاكِمٍ، وَتُثْبَتُ بَقِيَّةُ الأَحْكَامِ.

وَمَنْ رَآهُ وَحْدَهُ لِشَوَّالٍ لَمْ يُفْطِرْ، وَلِرَمَضَانَ وَرُدَّتْ شَهَادَتُهُ لَزِمَهُ الصَّومُ وَجَمِيعُ أَحْكَامِ الشَّهْرِ مِنْ طَلَاقٍ وَعِتَاقٍ وَغَيْرِهِمَا.

Obligations, Breaking the Fast, Intention

It is obligatory upon every capable Muslim of legal capacity. It is however required of every guardian to order the capable minor to fast, and smack them for it, in order that they become accustomed to it. Whoever is incapable, due to old age or terminal illness, is to break the fast and is obliged (unless coupled with a common excuse such as travel) to feed one poor person the amount which suffices an expiation for every day.

It is recommended to break the fast, and disliked maintain it, during a journey in which shortening is permitted, even if there is no difficulty. It is disliked for the pregnant and nursing women to fast while they fear for themselves or their child. They are to make up what they broke, and it is further required of someone feeding a child (while fearing for the child only), to feed a poor person for every day.

Breaking the fast is obligatory if required to save a sacred life from demise, such as drowning, etc. For every obligatory fast there must be a specific intention made at night, even if what contradicts it is done, but not the intention of mere obligation[86].

Voluntary fasting intended during the day (even after the zawāl), is valid, so long as nothing which spoils the fast has been previously committed. It is deemed as a legislated fast and will be rewarded from its time of commencement.

If someone conceives that they will fast tomorrow, they have made an intention, just like eating and drinking with the intention to fast[87].

---

86 The intention must be specifically for Ramaḍān and not a mere obligatory fast.

87 Eating and drinking at night in preparation to fast the following day.

فَصْلٌ

وَيَجِبُ عَلَى كُلِّ مُسْلِمٍ قَادِرٍ مُكَلَّفٍ، لَكِنْ عَلَى وَلِيِّ صَغِيرٍ مُطِيقٍ أَمْرُهُ بِهِ وَضَرْبُهُ عَلَيْهِ لِيَعْتَادَهُ، وَمَنْ عَجَزَ عَنْهُ لِكِبَرٍ أَوْ مَرَضٍ لَا يُرْجَى بُرْؤُهُ أَفْطَرَ وَعَلَيْهِ، لَا مَعَ عُذْرٍ مُعْتَادٍ كَسَفَرٍ، عَنْ كُلِّ يَوْمٍ لِمِسْكِينٍ مَا يُجْزِئُ فِي كَفَّارَةٍ.

وَسُنَّ فِطْرٌ، وَكُرِهَ صَوْمٌ بِسَفَرِ قَصْرٍ، وَلَوْ بِلَا مَشَقَّةٍ، وَكُرِهَ صَوْمُ حَامِلٍ وَمُرْضِعٍ خَافَتَا عَلَى أَنْفُسِهِمَا أَوْ الوَلَدِ، وَيَقْضِيَانِ مَا أَفْطَرَتَاهُ، وَيَلْزَمُ مَنْ يَمُونُ الوَلَدَ إِن خِيفَ عَلَيْهِ فَقَطْ إِطْعَامُ مِسْكِينٍ لِكُلِّ يَوْمٍ.

وَيَجِبُ الفِطْرُ عَلَى مَنْ اِحْتَاجَهُ لِإِنْقَاذِ مَعْصُومٍ مِنْ مَهْلَكَةٍ كَغَرَقٍ وَنَحْوِهِ، وَشُرِطَ لِكُلِّ يَوْمٍ وَاجِبٍ نِيَّةٌ مُعَيَّنَةٌ مِنَ اللَّيلِ وَلَوْ أَتَى بَعْدَهَا بِمُنَافٍ لَا نِيَّةُ الفَرْضِيَّةِ.

وَيَصِحُّ صَوْمُ نَفْلٍ مِمَّنْ لَمْ يَفْعَلْ مُفْسِداً بِنِيَّتِهِ نَهَاراً وَلَوْ بَعْدَ الزَّوَالِ، وَيُحْكَمُ بِالصَّوْمِ الشَّرْعِيِّ المُثَابِ عَلَيْهِ مِنْ وَقْتِهَا، وَمَنْ خَطَرَ بِقَلْبِهِ لَيْلاً أَنَّهُ صَائِمٌ غَداً فَقَدْ نَوَى، وَكَذَا الأَكْلُ وَالشُّرْبُ بِنِيَّةِ الصَّوْمِ.

Fast Invalidators

Whoever deliberately chooses to do the following, while aware they are fasting, will invalidate their fast: eat, drink, or apply eyeliner (which is known to reach the throat such as kuḥl etc.); insert something inside themselves; detect the flavor of gum[89] being chewed in the throat; swallow phlegm which reaches the mouth; induce vomiting; glance repeatedly or masturbate which stimulates ejaculation of orgasmic fluid; kiss, touch, or do intimate acts (without penetration) ejaculating either orgasmic or arousal fluids; or perform cupping, which draws blood, or has it done. It is not broken due to the following: phlebotomy or incision; thinking until ejaculation; any of the nullifiers of fasting being committed forgetfully or under duress; ingesting water used to clean the mouth and nose, even if it was exaggerated or done more than three times; unintentionally ingesting a fly or dust; or swallowing saliva that is gathered in the mouth.

[89] A traditional natural mastic gum with relatively no flavor. Chewing gum which dissolves during fasting hours is impermissible.

فَصْلٌ

وَمَنْ أَكَلَ أَوْ شَرِبَ أَوْ اِكْتَحَلَ بِمَا عَلِمَ وُصُولَهُ إِلَى حَلْقِهِ مِنْ كُحْلٍ وِنَحْوِهِ، أَوْ أَدْخَلَ إِلَى جَوْفِهِ شَيْئاً، أَوْ وَجَدَ طَعْمَ عِلْكٍ مَضَغَهُ بِحَلْقِهِ أَوْ وَصَلَ إِلَى فَمِهِ نُخَامَةٌ فَابْتَلَعَهَا، أَوْ اسْتَقَاءَ فَقَاءَ، أَوْ كَرَّرَ النَّظَرَ فَأَمْنَى أَوْ اسْتَمْنَى، أَوْ قَبَّلَ أَوْ لَمَسَ أَوْ بَاشَرَ دُونَ الفَرْجِ فَأَمْنَى أَوْ أَمْذَى، أَوْ حَجَمَ، أَوْ احْتَجَمَ وَظَهَرَ دَمٌ، عَامِداً مُخْتَاراً ذَاكِراً لِصَوْمِهِ أَفْطَرَ لَا بِفَصْدٍ وَشَرْطٍ، وَلَا إِنْ فَكَّرَ فَأَنْزَلَ، وَلَا إِنْ فَعَلَ شَيْئاً مِنْ جَمِيعِ المُفْطِرَاتِ نَاسِياً أَوْ مُكْرَهاً، وَلَا إِنْ دَخَلَ مَاءُ مَضْمَضَةٍ أَوْ اسْتِنْشَاقٍ حَلْقَهُ، وَلَوْ بَالَغَ أَوْ زَادَ عَلَى ثَلَاثٍ، وَلَا إِنْ دَخَلَ الذُّبَابُ أَوْ الغُبَارُ حَلْقَهُ بِغَيْرِ قَصْدٍ، وَلَا إِنْ جَمَعَ رِيقَهُ فَابْتَلَعَهُ.

Expiations & Recommended Acts

Whoever copulates (vaginally or anally) in the day (even with the deceased or a beast) while fasting, whether under duress or forgetful, must make it up and pay an expiation. The ruling is the same for whoever was voluntarily copulated with if they participated while neither ignorant nor forgetful. Whoever copulates one day and again during another and does not pay the expiation is required to pay a second expiation just like someone who repeats it in one day after paying. The expiation, only for copulation or ejaculation due to lesbian activity during the day of Ramaḍān, is manumission of a healthy bondservant. If one is not available, it is fasting two consecutive months, which if not possible, is feeding 60 poor people. If they are not available, it is voided, unlike the expiation for ḥajj, ẓihār, or an oath.

It is recommended to hasten to break the fast, say what has been narrated when breaking it, and delay the pre-dawn meal.

Whoever misses Ramaḍān is to make it up. It is recommended to do so immediately, except when there only remain the equivalent number of days in Shaʿbān that must be made up, in which case it becomes obligatory.

If required to make up Ramaḍān, it is not valid to begin voluntary fasting. Intending an obligatory fast or a make-up fast and then changing it to a voluntary fast is valid. It is impermissible to delay making up Ramaḍān until the next without an excuse. If done so, it is obligatory to also feed a poor person for every day. If such a squanderer were to die, food must be given from their wealth (even before the following Ramaḍān); it is not to be fasted on their behalf.

فَصْلٌ

وَمَنْ جَامَعَ فِي نَهَارٍ فِي قُبُلٍ أَوْ دُبُرٍ وَلَوْ لِمَيِّتٍ أَوْ بَهِيمَةٍ فِي حَالَةٍ يَلْزَمُهُ فِيهَا الإِمْسَاكُ مُكْرَهاً كَانَ أَوْ نَاسِياً لَزِمَهُ القَضَاءُ وَالكَفَّارَةُ، وَكَذَا مَنْ جُومِعَ إِنْ طَاوَعَ غَيْرَ جَاهِلٍ وَنَاسٍ، وَمَنْ جَامَعَ فِي يَوْمٍ ثُمَّ فِي آخَرٍ، وَلَمْ يُكَفِّرْ لَزِمَتْهُ ثَانِيَةٌ كَمَنْ أَعَادَهُ فِي يَوْمِهِ بَعْدَ أَنْ كَفَّرَ، وَلَا كَفَّارَةٌ بِغَيْرِ الجِمَاعِ وَالإِنْزَالِ بِالمُسَاحَقَةِ نَهَارَ رَمَضَانَ، وَهِيَ عِتْقُ رَقَبَةٍ مُؤْمِنَةٍ سَلِيمَةٍ، فَإِنْ لَمْ يَجِدْ فَصِيَامُ شَهْرَيْنِ مُتَتَابِعَيْنِ، فَإِنْ لَمْ يَسْتَطِعْ فَإِطْعَامُ سِتِّينَ مِسْكِيناً، فَإِنْ لَمْ يَجِدْ سَقَطَتْ بِخِلَافِ كَفَّارَةِ حَجٍّ أَوْ ظِهَارٍ أَوْ يَمِينٍ.

وَسُنَّ تَعْجِيلُ فِطْرٍ، وَتَأْخِيرُ سَحُورٍ، وَقَوْلُ مَا وَرَدَ عِنْدَ فِطْرٍ.

وَمَنْ فَاتَهُ رَمَضَانُ قَضَى عَدَدَ أَيَّامِهِ، وَيُسَنُّ عَلَى الفَوْرِ إِلَّا إِذَا بَقِيَ مِنْ شَعْبَانَ بِقَدْرِ مَا عَلَيْهِ فَيَجِبُ.

وَلَا يَصِحُّ ابْتِدَاءُ تَطَوُّعٍ مَنْ عَلَيْهِ قَضَاءُ رَمَضَانَ، فَإِنْ نَوَى صَوْماً وَاجِباً أَوْ قَضَاءً ثُمَّ قَلَبَهُ نَفْلاً صَحَّ. وَيَحْرُمُ تَأْخِيرُ قَضَاءِ رَمَضَانَ إِلَى آخَرٍ بِلَا عُذْرٍ، فَإِنْ فَعَلَ وَجَبَ مَعَ القَضَاءِ إِطْعَامُ مِسْكِينٍ عَنْ كُلِّ يَوْمٍ، وَإِنْ مَاتَ المُفَرِّطُ وَلَوْ قَبْلَ آخَرَ أُطْعِمَ عَنْهُ كَذَلِكَ مِنْ رَأْسِ مَالِهِ، وَلَا يُصَامُ عَنْهُ.

Voluntary Fasting

Voluntary fasts are recommended, the best of which are the following; every other day; three days of every month—the white days i.e. 13th, 14th, and 15th are best; Thursdays and Mondays; six days of Shawwāl (best to be done consecutively after ʿEid and when coupled with Ramaḍān are equivalent in reward to fasting the year); fasting Muḥarram[90] (both the ninth and especially the tenth which is an expiation for the year); and the 10 days of Dhul-Ḥijjah (especially the day of ʿArafah which is an expiation for two years).

The following are disliked to single out for fasting: Rajab[91]; Friday; Saturday; the day of doubt, i.e. the 30th of Shaʿbān (if there is no justification when it is time for the sighting); fasting Nayrūz[92] and Mahrajān[93]; every holiday of the disbelievers; any day singled out for veneration; and preceding Ramaḍān by one or two days, unless any of the above coincide with a habitual fast.

Fasting the days of tashrīq[94] is not valid unless done so for the ritual sacrifice of mutʿah or qirān[95]. There is absolutely no fasting on ʿEid, which is impermissible. Whoever begins a voluntary deed (besides ḥajj or ʿumrah), is recommended to complete it but not obliged. If it is nullified, it does not have to be made up. It is categorically obligatory to complete a compulsory act, even if its time is extensive, e.g. prayer, making up Ramaḍān, an oath, and an expiation. If it is invalidated, there is nothing extra to be done[96], nor is there an expiation.

The best day is Friday and the best night is Laylat al-Qadr (sought in the last 10 of Ramaḍān, particularly in their odd nights,

---

90 The first month of the Hijra calendar.

91 The seventh month of the Hijra calendar.

92 The fourth day of spring.

93 The 19th day of fall.

94 The 11th, 12th, and 13th of Dhul Ḥijjah.

95 Mutʿah and qirān and two different forms of ḥajj. Details to follow.

96 Besides repeating it or making it up.

فَصْلٌ

يُسَنُّ صَوْمُ التَطوُّعِ، وَأَفْضَلُه يومٌ وَيَوْمٌ، وصومُ ثَلَاثَةٍ مِنْ كُلِّ شَهْرٍ، وَأَيَّامُ البِيْضِ أَفْضَلُ، وَهِيَ ثَلَاثَ عَشْرَةَ وَأَرْبَعَ عَشْرَةَ وَخَمسَ عَشْرَةَ، وَالخَمِيسُ وَالاِثْنَيْنُ، وَسِتٌّ مِنْ شَوَّالٍ، وَالأَوْلَى تَتَابُعُهَا، وَعَقِبَ العِيْدِ، وَصَائِمُهَا مَعَ رَمَضَانَ كَأَنَّمَا صَامَ الدَّهْرَ، وَصَوْمُ المُحَرَّمِ، وآكَدُهُ العَاشِرُ، وَهُوَ كَفَّارَةُ سَنَةٍ، ثُمَّ التَّاسِعُ، وَعَشْرُ ذِي الحِجَّةِ، وآكَدُهُ يَوْمُ عَرَفَةَ، وَهُوَ كَفَّارَةُ سَنَتَيْنِ.

وَكُرِهَ إِفْرَادُ رَجَبٍ، وَالجُمُعَةِ، وَالسَّبْتِ بِصَوْمٍ، وَصَوْمُ يَومِ الشَّكِّ وَهُوَ الثَّلَاثُونَ مِنْ شَعْبَانَ إِذَا لَمْ يَكُنْ حِينَ التَّرَائِي عِلَّةٌ، وَصَوْمُ يَوْمِ النَّيْرُوزِ وَالمَهْرَجَانِ، وَكُلِّ عِيدٍ لِلْكُفَّارِ، أَوْ يَوْمٍ يُفْرِدُونَهُ بِتَعْظِيمٍ، وَتَقَدُّمُ رَمَضَانَ بِيومٍ أَوْ يومَينِ إِلَّا أَنْ يُوَافِقَ عَادَةً فِي الكُلِّ.

وَلَا يَصِحُّ صَوْمُ أَيَّامِ التَّشْرِيقِ إِلَّا عَنْ دَمِ مُتْعَةٍ أَوْ قِرَانٍ، وَلَا صَوْمُ عِيْدٍ مُطْلَقاً وَيَحْرُمُ، وَمَنْ دَخَلَ فِي تَطَوُّعٍ غَيْرِ حَجٍّ أَوْ عُمْرَةٍ لَمْ يَجِبْ إِتْمَامُهُ وَيُسَنُّ، وَإِنْ فَسَدَ فَلَا قَضَاءَ.

وَيَجِبُ إِتْمَامُ فَرْضٍ مَطْلَقاً وَلَوْ مُوَسَّعاً كَصَلَاةٍ، وَقَضَاءِ رَمَضَانَ، وَنَذْرٍ مُطْلَقٍ، وَكَفَّارَةٍ، وَإِنْ بَطَلَ فَلَا مَزِيدَ وَلَا كَفَّارَةَ.

وَأَفْضَلُ الأَيَّامِ يَوْمُ الجُمُعَةِ، وَأَفْضَلُ اللَّيَالِي لَيْلَةُ القَدْرِ، وَتُطْلَبُ فِي العَشْرِ الأَخِيرِ مِنْ رَمَضَانَ،

of which the most hopeful is the seventh). Abundant supplication should be made in them saying, "O Allāh, indeed you are oft-pardoning who loves to pardon, so pardon me."

وَأَوْتَارُهُ آكَدُ، وَأَرَجَاهَا سَابِعَتُهُ، وَيُكْثِرُ مِنْ دُعَائِهِ فِيهَا: "اللَّهُمَّ إِنَّكَ عَفُوٌّ تُحِبُّ العَفْوَ فَاعْفُ عَنِّي."

I'ttikāf

I'ttikāf[100] is recommended all the time, especially in Ramaḍān, in which the last 10 are more emphasized. It becomes obligatory due to a vow. Its prerequisites include the following: intention; Islām; sanity; discernment; and the absence of what necessitates ghusl. Additionally, it must be in a masjid that establishes congregational prayer for those required to attend. The masjid includes its expansion, its roof, its fenced courtyard, and its minaret (which either it, or its door, is within it)[101].

Whoever vows to make i'ttikāf, or perform prayer in a masjid other than the three, is permitted to do so in a different one. If they vowed to make it in one of them, they are permitted to do so in it or in a more virtuous one. The best of them is Masjid al-Ḥarām, then the Prophet's Masjid, then al-Aqṣā.

Whoever makes continual i'ttikāf due to a vow, is not to leave, except out of necessity. They are not to visit the sick, nor attend a funeral, unless stipulated. It is invalidated by the following: leaving the masjid without excuse; intending to leave (even if they do not); intercourse; ejaculation due to intimate acts; apostasy; and intoxication. Wherever it is invalidated, the continual non-time-specific type must be recommenced without expiation. That which is time-specific must be recommenced with an obligatory expiation for breaking an oath due to the loss of setting.

It is not invalidated for leaving the masjid to use the restroom, bring food, attend Jumu'ah (which is required), or perform some obligatory purification, etc. It is recommended to be busy with righteous deeds and refrain from what is of no concern. It is impermissible to make the Qur'ān a replacement for speech[102].

---

[100] The act of remaining sequestered in the masjid, if even for an hour, in a specific manner to perform acts of obedience.

[101] The minaret cannot be outside the masjid.

[102] Like seeing someone arrive on-time and saying, "Then you came at the decreed time, O Moses." (TaHa 20:40)

فَصْلٌ

وَالِاعْتِكَافُ سُنَّةٌ كُلَّ وَقْتٍ، وَفِي رَمَضَانَ آكَدُ، وَآكَدُهُ عَشْرُهُ الْأَخِيرُ.

وَيَجِبُ بِنَذْرٍ، وَشُرِطَ لَهُ نِيَّةٌ، وَإِسْلَامٌ، وَعَقْلٌ، وَتَمْيِيزٌ، وَعَدَمُ مَا يُوجِبُ الْغُسْلَ، وَكَوْنُهُ بِمَسْجِدٍ، وَيُزَادُ فِي حَقِّ مَنْ تَلْزَمُهُ الْجَمَاعَةُ أَنْ يَكُونَ الْمَسْجِدُ مِمَّا تُقَامُ فِيهِ، وَمِنَ الْمَسْجِدِ مَا زِيدَ فِيهِ، وَمِنْهُ ظَهْرُهُ، وَرَحْبَتُهُ الْمَحُوطَةُ، وَمَنَارَتُهُ الَّتِي هِيَ أَوْ بَابُهَا فِيهِ.

وَمَنْ نَذَرَ الِاعْتِكَافَ أَوِ الصَّلَاةَ فِي مَسْجِدٍ غَيْرِ الثَّلَاثَةِ فَلَهُ فِعْلُهُ فِي غَيْرِهِ، وَفِي أَحَدِهَا فَلَهُ فِعْلُهُ فِيهِ وَفِي الْأَفْضَلِ مِنْهُ، وَأَفْضَلُهَا الْمَسْجِدُ الْحَرَامُ، ثُمَّ مَسْجِدُ النَّبِيِّ ﷺ ثُمَّ الْأَقْصَى.

وَمَنِ اعْتَكَفَ مَنْذُوراً مُتَتَابِعاً لَمْ يَخْرُجْ إِلَّا لِمَا لَا بُدَّ مِنْهُ، وَلَا يَعُودُ مَرِيضاً، وَلَا يَشْهَدُ جَنَازَةً إِلَّا بِشَرْطٍ. وَيَبْطُلُ بِالْخُرُوجِ مِنَ الْمَسْجِدِ لِغَيْرِ عُذْرٍ، وَبِنِيَّةِ الْخُرُوجِ وَلَوْ لَمْ يَخْرُجْ، وَبِالْوَطْءِ فِي الْفَرْجِ، وَبِالْإِنْزَالِ بِالْمُبَاشَرَةِ دُونَ الْفَرْجِ، وَبِالرِّدَّةِ، وَبِالسُّكْرِ، وَحَيْثُ بَطَلَ وَجَبَ اسْتِئْنَافُ الْمُتَتَابِعِ غَيْرِ الْمُقَيَّدِ بِزَمَنٍ وَلَا كَفَّارَةَ. وَإِنْ كَانَ مُقَيَّداً بِزَمَنٍ مُعَيَّنٍ اسْتَأْنَفَهُ، وَعَلَيْهِ كَفَّارَةُ يَمِينٍ لِفَوَاتِ الْمَحَلِّ.

وَلَا يَبْطُلُ إِنْ خَرَجَ مِنَ الْمَسْجِدِ لِبَوْلٍ أَوْ غَائِطٍ أَوْ إِتْيَانٍ بِمَأْكَلٍ وَمَشْرَبٍ أَوْ لِجُمُعَةٍ تَلْزَمُهُ أَوْ طَهَارَةٍ وَاجِبَةٍ وَنَحْوِ ذَلِكَ.

وَيُسَنُّ تَشَاغُلُهُ بِالْقُرَبِ، وَاجْتِنَابُ مَا لَا يَعْنِيهِ، وَيَحْرُمُ جَعْلُ الْقُرْآنِ بَدَلاً مِنَ الْكَلَامِ،

When going to the masjid, iʿttikāf should be intended for the duration they remain there.

وَيِنْبَغِي لِمَنْ قَصَدَ المَسْجِدَ أَنْ يِنَوِيَ الِاعْتِكَافَ مُدَّةَ لُبْثِهِ فِيهِ.

Ḥajj

It is a communal obligation every year. It is to go to Makkah to perform specific acts at specific times and is a pillar of Islām. ʿUmrah is to visit the house in a specific manner. Both are obligatory once in a lifetime based on five prerequisites, which include: Islām; sanity (it is not valid from a disbeliever or the insane even if the guardian were to make iḥrām[104] on their behalf); puberty; and complete freedom (it is valid for a minor or a bondservant).

The minor's guardian is to make iḥrām on their behalf. It will not suffice either of them for their obligatory ḥajj or ʿumrah.

If a minor reaches puberty, or a bondservant is manumitted, before 'the standing' or after it (and they return within enough time), it will suffice their obligatory ḥajj.

The fifth is capability i.e. owning provisions and suitable transport, or possession of what is enough to obtain it, so long as it is in addition to what is required of books, dwellings, servants, and both personal and familial expenses necessary for survival.

Whoever meets these prerequisites is immediately required to go, so long as the way is safe. If they are unable to go due to old age or chronic illness, a free proxy (even if female) must perform both on their behalf if they are obligations. It is not valid for someone who has not completed ḥajj to perform the obligatory, vowed, or voluntary ḥajj on behalf of another. If they do so, it will be counted as their own obligatory ḥajj. There is an additional sixth prerequisite for females; they must find a husband or maḥram of legal capacity who can afford both their provisions and transport. If they are not able, they are to appoint a proxy. If they make ḥajj without a maḥram it is considered valid though impermissible.

[104] Defined in the chapter entitled Iḥrām & Ḥajj Types.

كِتَابُ الحَجِّ

وَهُوَ فَرْضُ كِفَايَةٍ كُلَّ عَامٍ، وَهُوَ قَصْدُ مَكَّةَ لِعَمَلٍ مَخْصُوصٍ فِي زَمَنٍ مَخْصُوصٍ، وَهُوَ أَحَدُ أَرْكَانِ الإِسْلَامِ. وَالعُمْرَةُ زِيَارَةُ البَيْتِ عَلَى وَجْهٍ مَخْصُوصٍ. وَيَجِبَانِ فِي العُمْرِ مَرَّةً بِخَمْسَةِ شُرُوطٍ: وَهِيَ الإِسْلَامُ، وَالعَقْلُ، فَلَا يَصِحَّانِ مِنْ كَافِرٍ وَمَجْنُونٍ وَلَوْ أَحْرَمَ عَنْهُ وَلِيُّهُ، وَالبُلُوغُ، وَكَمَالُ الحُرِيَّةِ، لَكِنْ يَصِحَّانِ مِنَ الصَّغِيرِ وَالرَّقِيقِ، وَيُحْرِمُ عَنِ الصَّغِيرِ وَلِيُّهُ، وَلَا يُجْزِئَانِ عَنْ حَجَّةِ الإِسْلَامِ وَعُمْرَتِهِ، فَإِنْ بَلَغَ الصَّغِيرُ أَوْ عَتِقَ الرَّقِيقُ قَبْلَ الوُقُوفِ أَوْ بَعْدَهُ إِنْ أَعَادَ فَوَقَفَ فِي وَقْتِهِ أَجْزَأَهُ عَنْ حَجَّةِ الإِسْلَامِ، وَالخَامِسُ الاِسْتِطَاعَةُ، وَهِيَ مِلْكُ زَادٍ وَرَاحِلَةٍ تَصْلُحُ لِمِثْلِهِ، أَوْ مِلْكُ مَا يَقْدِرُ بِهِ عَلَى تَحْصِيلِ ذَلِكَ بِشَرْطِ كَوْنِهِ فَاضِلاً عَمَّا يَحْتَاجُهُ مِنْ كُتُبٍ وَمَسْكَنٍ وَخَادِمٍ، وَعَنْ مُؤْنَتِهِ وَمُؤْنَةِ عِيَالِهِ عَلَى الدَّوَامِ.

فَمَنْ كَمُلَتْ لَهُ هَذِهِ الشُّرُوطُ لَزِمَهُ السَّعْيُ فَوْراً إِنْ كَانَ فِي الطَّرِيقِ أَمْنٌ، فَإِنْ عَجَزَ عَنْهُ لِكِبَرٍ أَوْ مَرَضٍ لَا يُرْجَى بُرْؤُهُ لَزِمَهُ أَنْ يُقِيمَ نَائِباً حُرّاً وَلَوْ اِمْرَأَةً يَحُجُّ وَيَعْتَمِرُ عَنْهُ مِنْ حَيْثُ وَجَبَا، وَلَا يَصِحُّ مِمَّنْ لَمْ يَحُجَّ عَنْ نَفْسِهِ حَجٌّ عَنْ فَرْضِ غَيْرِهِ، وَلَا عَنْ نَذْرٍ وَلَا نَافِلَةٍ، فَإِنْ فَعَلَ انْصَرَفَ إِلَى حَجَّةِ الإِسْلَامِ، وَتَزِيدُ الأُنْثَى شَرْطاً سَادِساً وَهُوَ أَنْ تَجِدَ لَهَا زَوْجاً أَوْ مَحْرَماً مُكَلَّفاً، وَأَنْ تَقْدِرَ عَلَى الزَّادِ وَالرَّاحِلَةِ لَهَا وَلَهُ، فَإِنْ أَيِسَتْ مِنْهُ اسْتَنَابَتْ، وَإِنْ حَجَّتْ بِلَا مَحْرَمٍ حَرُمَ وَأَجْزَأَ.

Miqāts

The miqāts are specified places and times for specific acts of worship. The Miqāt for Madīnah is Dhul-Ḥulayfa, for the Levant, Egypt, and the west is Juḥfa, for Yemen is Yalamlam, for the highlands of the Ḥijāz, the highlands of Yemen, and Tā'if is Qarn, and for the east is Dhāt ʿIrq. These are for their respective inhabitants and all who pass by. The miqāt of whoever's dwelling is closer than them is their dwelling itself. Whoever is in Makkah, is to make iḥrām for ḥajj there. It is valid from outside sacred grounds without a blood sacrifice. Iḥrām for ʿumrah is made from outside sacred grounds. It is valid from Makkah but requires a blood sacrifice.

فَصْلٌ

وَالْمَوَاقِيتُ مَوَاضِعُ وَأَزْمِنَةٌ مُعَيَّنَةٌ لِعِبَادَةٍ مَخْصُوصَةٍ، فَمِيقَاتُ أَهْلِ الْمَدِينَةِ ذُو الْحُلَيْفَةِ،

وَالشَّامِ وَمِصْرَ وَالْمَغْرِبِ الْجُحْفَةُ، وَالْيَمَنِ يَلَمْلَمُ، وَنَجْدِ الْحِجَازِ وَالْيَمَنِ وَالطَّائِفِ قَرْنُ،

وَالْمَشْرِقِ ذَاتُ عِرْقٍ، وَهَذِهِ لِأَهْلِهَا وَلِمَنْ مَرَّ عَلَيْهَا، وَمَنْ مَنْزِلُهُ دُونَهَا فَمِيقَاتُهُ مِنْهُ.

وَيُحْرِمُ مَنْ بِمَكَّةَ لِحَجٍّ مِنْهَا، وَيَصِحُّ مِنَ الْحِلِّ وَلَا دَمَ عَلَيْهِ، وَلِعُمْرَةٍ مِنَ الْحِلِّ، وَيَصِحُّ

مِنْ مَكَّةَ وَعَلَيْهِ دَمٌ.

Iḥrām & Ḥajj Types

It is recommended for anyone wishing to make iḥrām, i.e. the intention for the rites, to: perform ghusl or tayummum to cleanse themselves; to perfume their body (which is disliked on the clothing); and for men to wear two clean white coverings, one upper and one lower, after removing all fitted clothing. Iḥrām is made after a compulsory or two-rakʿah voluntary prayer (outside of the prohibited times). Its intention is a prerequisite.

The best type is tamattuʿ i.e. to make iḥrām for ʿumrah during the months of ḥajj and then after its completion to make iḥrām for ḥajj. Ifrād is to make iḥrām for ḥajj and then after its completion to make iḥrām for ʿumrah. Qirān is to make iḥrām for both together or to make iḥrām for ʿumrah and then add it[105] before beginning its ṭawāf.

It is recommended to specify a ritual type and to make it conditional, saying, "O Allāh I desire *such and such* ritual, so facilitate it for me and accept it from me and if I were to be prevented by something, then my place of disengagement is wherever I am prevented". If it is made, it is not voided, and thus must be completed and made up.

---

[105] The intention for ḥajj with ʿumrah.

فَصْلٌ

وَسُنَّ لِمُرِيدِ الإِحْرَامِ، وَهُوَ نِيَّةُ النُّسُكِ، غُسْلٌ أَوْ تَيَمُّمٌ وَتَنَظُّفٌ، وَتَطَيُّبٌ فِي بَدَنٍ، وَكُرِهَ فِي ثَوْبٍ، وَلُبسُ إِزَارٍ وَرِدَاءٍ أَبْيَضَيْنِ نَظِيفَيْنِ بَعْدَ تَجَرُّدِ ذَكَرٍ عَنْ مَخِيطٍ، وَإِحْرَامُهُ عَقِبَ صَلَاةِ فَرْضٍ أَوْ رَكْعَتَيْنِ نَفْلاً فِي غَيْرِ وَقْتِ نَهْيٍ، وَنِيَّتُهُ شَرْطٌ.

وَأَفْضَلُ الأَنْسَاكِ التَّمَتُّعُ، وَهُوَ أَنْ يُحْرِمَ بِالعُمْرَةِ فِي أَشْهُرِ الحَجِّ، ثُمَّ بَعْدَ فَرَاغِهِ مِنْهَا يُحْرِمُ بِالحَجِّ، وَالإِفْرَادُ أَنْ يُحْرِمَ بِالحَجِّ ثُمَّ بَعْدَ فَرَاغِهِ مِنْهُ يُحْرِمُ بِالعُمْرَةِ، وَالقِرَانُ أَنْ يُحْرِمَ بِهِمَا مَعاً أَوْ يُحْرِمَ بِالعُمْرَةِ ثُمَّ يُدْخِلُهُ عَلَيْهَا قَبْلَ الشُّرُوعِ فِي طَوَافِهَا.

وَسُنَّ أَنْ يُعَيِّنَ نُسُكاً، وَأَنْ يَشْتَرِطَ فَيَقُولُ: اللَّهُمَّ إِنِّي أُرِيدُ النُّسُكَ الفُلَانِيَّ فَيَسِّرْهُ لِي، وَتَقَبَّلْهُ مِنِّي، وَإِنْ حَبَسَنِي حَابِسٌ فَمَحِلِّي حَيْثُ حَبَسْتَنِي، وَإِذَا انْعَقَدَ لَمْ يَبْطُلْ، بَلْ يَلْزَمُهُ إِتْمَامُهُ وَالقَضَاءُ.

Prohibitions of Iḥrām

There are nine prohibitions of iḥrām which are: removing hair; clipping finger or toe nails; covering the head of a male; a male wearing fitted clothing (except for pants in the absence of a waist wrap and khuffs in the absence of sandals); applying perfume; killing a consumable land game animal; what it begets; and what is begotten from cross-breading; entering a marriage contract; intercourse; and other intimate acts.

For all the prohibitions there are expiations, except for killing lice and entering a marriage contract. The local value for eggs and locusts must be paid. The expiation of a single hair and nail is feeding a poor person and that of two, is two. Necessity knows no law for the muḥrim[106], however they must offer an expiation.

---

[106] Someone in the state of iḥrām.

فَصْلٌ

وَمَحْظُورَاتُ الْإِحْرَامِ تِسْعٌ: إِزَالَةُ شَعْرٍ، وَتَقْلِيمُ ظُفْرِ يَدٍ أَوْ رِجْلٍ، وَتَغْطِيَةُ رَأْسِ ذَكَرٍ،

وَلُبْسُهُ الْمَخِيطَ إِلَّا سَرَاوِيلَ لِعَدَمِ إِزَارٍ، وَخُفَّيْنِ لِعَدَمِ نَعْلَيْنِ، وَالطِّيبُ، وَقَتْلُ صَيْدِ الْبَرِّ

الْوَحْشِيِّ الْمَأْكُولِ، وَالْمُتَوَلِّدِ مِنْهُ وَمِنْ غَيْرِهِ، وَعَقْدُ نِكَاحٍ، وَجِمَاعٌ، وَمُبَاشَرَةٌ فِيمَا دُونَ

الْفَرْجِ. وَفِي جَمِيعِ الْمَحْظُورَاتِ الْفِدْيَةُ إِلَّا قَتْلَ الْقَمْلِ وَعَقْدَ النِّكَاحِ، وَفِي الْبَيْضِ وَالْجَرَادِ

قِيمَتُهُ مَكَانَهُ، وَفِي الشَّعْرَةِ أَوِ الظُّفْرِ إِطْعَامُ مِسْكِينٍ، وَفِي الِاثْنَيْنِ إِطْعَامُ اثْنَيْنِ،

وَالضَّرُورَاتُ تُبِيحُ لِلْمُحْرِمِ الْمَحْظُورَاتِ وَيَفْدِي.

Expiations

It is what is obligatory due to iḥrām or the Ḥaram. The expiation of shaving; removing more than two hairs or nails; applying perfume; wearing fitted clothes; a male covering his head; or a woman covering her face, is to choose between fasting three days, feeding six poor people one mudd[107] of wheat or one-half ṣāʿ of something else, or slaughtering a sheep. The compensation for hunting is to choose between an analogous animal or appraising its value in dirhams and purchasing food sufficient for fiṭr to feed every poor person one mudd of wheat or one-half ṣāʿ of something else; or fasting one day in place of the food for each poor person. For the non-analogous animal, it is between feeding or fasting.

If the mutamattiʿ[108] or qārin[109] is unable to procure a sacrificial animal, they must fast three days during ḥajj (making the last of them the day of ʿArafah is best) and then seven days upon their return home. If someone who is restricted is unable to obtain one, they must fast 10 days and then disengage. It is not required for heedlessly wearing fitted clothing, applying perfume, or covering the head.

Every sacrificial animal or feeding belongs to the poor people of the Ḥaram, except for the expiations given for shaving the head, fitted clothing, etc., which are to be distributed wherever their causes are found. Fasting is valid in every place. The blood sacrifice is either one sheep or one-seventh of a camel or cow.

---

[107] Approximately 0.608 liters.

[108] Someone performing tamattuʿ.

[109] Someone performing qirān.

فَصْلٌ فِي الفِدْيَةِ

وَهِيَ مَا يَجِبُ بِسَبَبِ إِحْرَامٍ أَوْ حَرَمٍ، فَيُخَيَّرُ بِفِدْيَةِ حَلْقٍ وَإِزَالَةِ أَكْثَرَ مِنْ شَعْرَتَيْنِ أَوْ ظُفْرَيْنِ، وَطِيبٍ، وَلُبْسِ مَخِيطٍ، وَتَغْطِيَةِ رَأْسِ ذَكَرٍ وَوَجْهِ امْرَأَةٍ بَيْنَ صِيَامِ ثَلَاثَةِ أَيَّامٍ أَوْ إِطْعَامِ سِتَّةِ مَسَاكِينَ، كُلَّ مِسْكِينٍ مُدَّ بُرٍّ، أَوْ نِصْفَ صَاعٍ مِنْ غَيْرِهِ، أَوْ ذَبْحِ شَاةٍ. وَفِي جَزَاءِ صَيْدٍ بَيْنَ مِثْلِ مِثْلِيٍّ أَوْ تَقْوِيمِهِ بِدَرَاهِمَ يَشْتَرِي بِهَا طَعَاماً يُجْزِئُ فِي فِطْرَةٍ، فَيُطْعِمُ كُلَّ مِسْكِينٍ مُدَّ بُرٍّ، أَوْ نِصْفَ صَاعٍ مِنْ غَيْرِهِ، أَوْ يَصُومُ عَنْ طَعَامِ كُلِّ مِسْكِينٍ يَوْماً، وَبَيْنَ إِطْعَامٍ أَوْ صِيَامٍ فِي غَيْرِ مِثْلِيٍّ.

وَإِنْ عَدِمَ مُتَمَتِّعٌ أَوْ قَارِنٌ الهَدْيَ صَامَ ثَلَاثَةَ أَيَّامٍ فِي الحَجِّ، وَالأَفْضَلُ جَعْلُ آخِرِهَا يَوْمَ عَرَفَةَ وَسَبْعَةً إِذَا رَجَعَ إِلَى أَهْلِهِ، وَالمُحْصَرُ إِذَا لَمْ يَجِدْهُ صَامَ عَشَرَةَ أَيَّامٍ، ثُمَّ حَلَّ، وَتَسْقُطُ بِنِسْيَانٍ فِي لُبْسٍ وَطِيبٍ وَتَغْطِيَةِ رَأْسٍ. وَكُلُّ هَدْيٍ أَوْ إِطْعَامٍ فَلِمَسَاكِينِ الحَرَمِ إِلَّا فِدْيَةَ أَذًى وَلُبْسٍ وَنَحْوِهِمَا، فَحَيْثُ وُجِدَ سَبَبُهَا، وَيُجْزِئُ الصَّوْمُ بِكُلِّ مَكَانٍ، وَالدَّمُ شَاةٌ أَوْ سُبْعُ بَدَنَةٍ أَوْ بَقَرَةٍ.

Appraisal of Game Animals

They are of two categories: that which has an analogous livestock animal (which is obligatory and is of two types: the first is what the companions adjudicated which includes ostrich—for which is a camel; zebra, antelope, deer, hartebeest, and ibex—for which is a cow; aardwolf[112]—for which is a sheep; gazelle—for which is a sheep; hyrax and lizard—for which is a kid; jerboa—for which is a four month she-goat; rabbit—for which is a she-kid less than a she-goat; and ḥamām i.e. every type of bird that drinks water and coos—for which there is a sheep) and the second which is what the companions did not adjudicate and should be referred to the judgement of two upright specialists.

The second category is that which does not have an analogous type and includes the remaining species of birds, for which is their local value.

112 The word ḍabʿ is often translated as hyena, a carnivorous beast of prey that possesses canine teeth, which fits the description of impermissible animals. The aardwolf, an extant species of the hyena, does possess canine teeth but is insectivorous and therefore does not scavenge or kill animals. It is most likely that the aardwolf is what is being referred to as it is not considered a carnivorous beast of prey. Further details can be found in the works of Ibn al-Qayyim such as Iʿlām al-Muwaqqiʿīn.

فَصْلٌ فِي جَزَاءِ الصَّيدِ

وَهُوَ ضَرْبَانِ: مَا لَهُ مِثْلٌ مِنَ النَّعَمِ، فَيَجِبُ فِيهِ ذَلِكَ المِثْلُ.

وَهُوَ نَوْعَانِ: أَحَدُهُمَا: قَضَتْ فِيهِ الصَّحَابَةُ، وَمِنْهُ فِي النَّعَامَةِ بَدَنَةٌ، وَفِي حِمَارِ الوَحْشِ وَبَقَرِهِ وَأُيَّلٍ وَثَيْتَلٍ وَوَعِلٍ بَقَرَةٌ، وَفِي الضَّبعِ كَبْشٌ، وَفِي الغَزَالِ شَاةٌ، وَفِي الوَبْرِ وَالضَّبِّ جَدْيٌ، وَفِي اليَرْبُوعِ جَفْرَةٌ لَهَا أَرْبَعَةُ أَشْهُرٍ، وَفِي الأَرْنَبِ عَنَاقٌ دُونَ الجَفْرَةِ، وَفِي الحَمَامِ، وَهُوَ كُلُّ مَا عَبَّ المَاءَ وَهَدَرَ، شَاةٌ. النَّوعُ الثَّانِي: مَا لَمْ تَقْضِ فِيهِ الصَّحَابَةُ، وَيُرْجَعُ فِيهِ إِلَى قَوْلِ عَدْلَيْنِ خَبِيرَيْنِ.

الضَّرْبُ الثَّانِي: مَا لَا مِثْلَ لَهُ، وَهُوَ بَاقِي الطَّيْرِ وَفِيهِ قِيمَتُهُ مَكَانَهُ.

Sanctuary of Makkah & Madinah

Hunting in the sanctuary of Makkah is impermissible and its ruling is like hunting while in iḥrām. The following are impermissible to cut trees; grass (even thorns which may cause harm); siwāk, etc.; and leaves (but not dried leaves, sweet grass, truffles, mushrooms, fruit, and whatever is planted by man—including trees).

It is permissible to pasture its grass and benefit from what has died or broken, without human interference, even if it is not completely separated.

A small (per custom) tree warrants a sheep; what is larger warrants a cow. A choice is made between that and its estimated value—the price of which is treated like the recompense of hunting. Grass warrants its market value.

It is disliked remove dirt and rocks, but not zamzam water, from the sanctuary to non-sacred land.

It is recommended to reside in Makkah, which is more virtuous than Madinah. Both good and evil deeds are multiplied in virtuous places and during virtuous times. It is impermissible to hunt in the sanctuary of Madinah and to cut its trees and grass, except for need of fodder and small saddles, etc., which has no recompense.

فَصْلٌ

وَحَرُمَ صَيْدُ حَرَمِ مَكَّةَ، وَحُكْمُهُ حُكْمُ صِيدِ الإِحْرَامِ، وَحَرُمَ قَطْعُ شَجَرِهِ وَحَشِيشِهِ حَتَّى الشَوْكِ وَلَوْ ضَرَّ، وَالسِّوَاكِ وَنَحْوِهِ، وَالوَرَقِ إِلَّا اليَابِسَ وَالإِذْخِرَ، وَالكَمْأَةَ وَالفَقْعَ وَالثَّمَرَةَ، وَمَا زَرَعَهُ آدَمِيٌّ حَتَّى مِنَ الشَّجَرِ.

وَيُبَاحُ رَعْيُ حَشِيشِهِ، وَانْتِفَاعٌ بِمَا زَالَ أَوْ انْكَسَرَ بِغَيْرِ فِعْلِ آدَمِيٍّ وَلَوْ لَمْ يَبِنْ.

وَتُضْمَنُ الشَّجَرَةُ الصَّغِيرَةُ عُرْفاً بِشَاةٍ، وَمَا فَوْقَهَا بِبَقَرَةٍ، وَيُخَيَّرُ بَيْنَ ذَلِكَ وَبَيْنَ تَقْوِيمِهِ، وَيَفْعَلُ بِقِيمَتِهِ كَجَزَاءِ صَيْدٍ، وَحَشِيشٌ بِقِيمَتِهِ.

وَكُرِهَ إِخْرَاجُ تُرَابِ الحَرَمِ وَحِجَارَتِهِ إِلَى الحِلِّ إِلَّا مَاءُ زَمْزَمَ.

وَتُسْتَحَبُّ المُجَاوَرَةُ بِمَكَّةَ، وَهِيَ أَفْضَلُ مِنَ المَدِينَةِ، وَتُضَاعَفُ الحَسَنَةُ وَالسَّيِّئَةُ بِمَكَانٍ وَزَمَانٍ فَاضِلٍ. وَحَرُمَ صَيْدُ حَرَمِ المَدِينَةِ، وَقَطْعُ شَجَرِهِ وَحَشِيشِهِ لِغَيْرِ حَاجَةِ عَلَفٍ وَقَتَبٍ وَنَحْوِهِمَا وَلَا جَزَاءَ.

Entering Makkah

It is recommended to enter during the day from its peak i.e. the Gap of Kadāʾ, and to exit from its base i.e. the Gap of Kudā. The masjid should be entered from the door of Banī Shaybah. Whoever sees the Kaʿbah is to raise their hands and say what has been narrated followed by ṭawāf for ʿumrah as a mutamattiʿ or for arrival as a mufrid or qārin. Men should tuck the middle of the top wrap under their right shoulder in all seven circuits, unless carrying someone excused.

It is begun at the black stone, facing it (or a part thereof) with the entire body, then it is touched with the right hand, kissed, and prostrated upon. If that is difficult, it is touched with the hand and kissed; thronging should be avoided. If that is difficult, it is touched with something which is then kissed. If that is difficult, a gesture with the hand or something is made (without kissing it) while directing the face to it and saying what is narrated.

Then with the Kaʿbah on the left side, those coming from far away jog with short strides in the ṭawāf. Upon completion, two rakʿahs are prayed, which are best done behind al-Maqām[113]; an obligatory prayer will suffice instead. Then the stone is touched, exit for saʿī[114] is made from the door of Ṣafā, which is climbed until the Kaʿbah is seen, then takbīr is made three times and what has been narrated is said. Then they descend, walking to the first marker, and then run until they reach the next marker. They then walk and climb Marwah and say what they did on Ṣafā.

Then they walk back and run, where running is prescribed, to Ṣafā; doing it seven times. Each departure from Ṣafā is counted as one lap and each return to Ṣafā is counted as another. It begins at Ṣafā and ends at Marwah. Beginning from Marwah does not count as a lap.

---

[113] Maqām Ibrāhīm.

[114] The ceremony of running seven times between Ṣafā and Marwah.

بَابُ دُخُولِ مَكَّةَ

يُسَنُّ نَهاراً مِنْ أَعْلاَهَا مِنْ ثَنِيَّةِ كَدَاءٍ، وَخُرُوجٌ مِنْ أَسْفَلِهَا مِنْ ثَنِيَّةِ كُدَى، وَدُخُولُ المَسْجِدِ مِنْ بَابِ بَنِي شَيْبَةَ، فَإِذَا رَأَى البَيْتَ رَفَعَ يَدَيْهِ وَقَالَ مَا وَرَدَ، ثُمَّ يَطُوفُ مُتَمَتِّعٌ لِلْعُمْرَةِ وَمُفْرِدٌ وَقَارِنٌ لِلْقُدُومِ وَهُوَ الوُرُودُ، وَيَضْطَبِعُ غَيْرُ حَامِلٍ مَعْذُورٍ فِي كُلِّ أُسْبُوعِهِ،

وَيَبْتَدِئُهُ مِنَ الحَجَرِ الأَسْوَدِ فَيُحَاذِيهِ أَوْ بَعْضَهُ بِكُلِّ بَدَنِهِ، وَيَسْتَلِمُهُ بِيَدِهِ اليُمْنَى وَيُقَبِّلُهُ وَيَسْجُدُ عَلَيْهِ، فَإِنْ شَقَّ لَمْ يُزَاحِمْ، وَاسْتَلَمَهُ بِيَدِهِ وَقَبَّلَهَا، فَإِنْ شَقَّ فَبِشَيْءٍ وَقَبَّلَهُ، فَإِنْ شَقَّ أَشَارَ إِلَيْهِ بِيَدِهِ أَوْ بِشَيْءٍ وَلَا يُقَبِّلُهُ، وَاسْتَقْبَلَهُ بِوَجْهِهِ وَقَالَ مَا وَرَدَ.

ثُمَّ يَجْعَلُ البَيْتَ عَنْ يَسَارِهِ، وَيَرْمُلُ الأُفُقِيُّ فِي هَذَا الطَّوَافِ، فَإِذَا فَرَغَ صَلَّى رَكْعَتَيْنِ، وَالأَفْضَلُ كَوْنُهُمَا خَلْفَ المَقَامِ، وَتُجْزِئُ مَكْتُوبَةٌ عَنْهُمَا، ثُمَّ يَسْتَلِمُ الحَجَرَ وَيَخْرُجُ لِلسَّعْيِ مِنْ بَابِ الصَّفَا فَيَرْقَاهُ حَتَّى يَرَى البَيْتَ فَيُكَبِّرُ ثَلَاثاً وَيَقُولُ مَا وَرَدَ، ثُمَّ يَنْزِلُ مَاشِياً إِلَى العَلَمِ الأَوَّلِ فَيَسْعَى سَعْياً شَدِيداً إِلَى العَلَمِ الآخَرِ،

ثُمَّ يَمْشِي وَيَرْقَى المَرْوَةَ وَيَقُولُ مَا قَالَهُ عَلَى الصَّفَا، ثُمَّ يَنْزِلُ فَيَمْشِي فِي مَوْضِعِ مَشْيِهِ وَيَسْعَى فِي مَوْضِعِ سَعْيِهِ إِلَى الصَّفَا، يَفْعَلُهُ سَبْعاً، وَيَحْسِبُ ذَهَابَهُ سَعْيَةً وَرُجُوعَهُ سَعْيَةً، يَفْتَتِحُ بِالصَّفَا وَيَخْتِمُ بِالمَرْوَةِ، فَإِنْ بَدَأَ بِالمَرْوَةِ لَمْ يَحْتَسِبْ بِذَلِكَ الشَّوْطِ.

Description of Ḥajj & ʿUmrah

It is recommended for those in Makkah, from outside the sanctuary, to make iḥrām for ḥajj on the day of tarwiyah (the 8th of Dhul-Ḥijjah) and to sleep in Minā. After the sun rises, they leave for, and stay in, Namirah until the zawāl. Then they move to ʿArafah, which is entirely a place of standing except Baṭna ʿUranah, i.e. from the mount overseeing ʿArafah to its opposing mountains and the walls of Banī ʿĀmir. They are to combine ẓuhr and ʿaṣr at the time of ẓuhr.

It is recommended to stay their mounted (unlike the remaining rites), while facing the qiblah close to the boulders and Mt. Raḥmah, which is not legislated to climb on. They raise their hands and make abundant supplication from what has been narrated.

The time of 'standing' is from fajr of ʿArafah until the day of sacrifice's fajr. Afterwards they tranquilly go, post-sunset, to Muzdalifah and combine maghrib and ʿishāʾ at the time of ʿishāʾ and stay there for the night. After praying the morning prayer, they go to Mash'ar al-Ḥarām[117], climb it and stand there praising, unifying, and extolling Allāh, supplicating from what has narrated, and reciting the two verses 198 and 199, "But when you depart from ʿArafah, remember Allāh at al-Mash'ar al-Ḥaram...".

They then supplicate until the light of dawn and proceed to Minā. Upon reaching Muḥassir[118], they quickly go a stone's throw and take 70 pebbles (bigger than chick-peas but smaller than hazelnuts) for stoning, from wherever they wish. Taking them from the sanctuary, the weeds, or to breaking them is disliked

It is not recommended to wash them. Pebbles soiled with najāsah will suffice, though they are disliked.

---

[117] A small mountain in Muzdalifah, named as such due to it being a sign of ḥajj.

[118] Located between Muzdalifah and Minā.

فَصْلٌ فِي صِفَةِ الحَجِّ وَالعُمْرَةِ

يُسَنُّ لِمُحِلٍّ بِمَكَّةَ الإِحْرَامُ بِالحَجِّ يَوْمَ التَّرْوِيَةِ وَهُوَ الثَّامِنُ مِنْ ذِي الحِجَّةِ، وَالمَبِيتُ بِمِنَى، فَإِذَا طَلَعَتْ الشَّمْسُ سَارَ فَأَقَامَ إِلَى الزَّوَالِ، ثُمَّ يَأْتِي عَرَفَةَ وَكُلُّهَا مَوْقِفٌ إِلَّا بَطْنَ عُرَنَةَ، وَهُوَ الجَبَلُ المُشْرِفُ عَلَى عَرَفَةَ إِلَى الجِبَالِ المُقَابِلَةِ لَهُ إِلَى مَا يَلِي حَوَائِطَ بَنِي عَامِرٍ، وَيَجْمَعُ فِيهَا بَيْنَ الظُّهْرِ وَالعَصْرِ تَقْدِيماً.

وَسُنَّ وُقُوفُهُ رَاكِباً بِخِلَافِ سَائِرِ المَنَاسِكِ، مُسْتَقْبِلَ القِبْلَةَ عِنْدَ الصَّخْرَاتِ وَجَبَلِ الرَّحْمَةِ، وَلَا يُشْرَعُ صُعُودُهُ، وَيَرْفَعُ يَدَيْهِ، وَيُكْثِرُ الدُّعَاءَ بِمَا وَرَدَ. وَوَقْتُ الوُقُوفِ مِنْ فَجْرِ عَرَفَةَ إِلَى فَجْرِ يَوْمِ النَّحْرِ، ثُمَّ يَدْفَعُ بَعْدَ الغُرُوبِ إِلَى مُزْدَلِفَةَ بِسَكِينَةٍ، وَيَجْمَعُ فِيهَا بَيْنَ العِشَائَيْنِ تَأْخِيراً وَيَبِيتُ بِهَا، فَإِذَا صَلَّى الصُّبْحَ أَتَى المَشْعَرَ الحَرَامَ، فَرَقَاهُ وَوَقَفَ عِنْدَهُ، وَحَمِدَ اللَّهَ تَعَالَى وَهَلَّلَ وَكَبَّرَ، وَدَعَا بِمَا وَرَدَ وَقَرَأَ: (فَإِذَا أَفَضْتُمْ مِنْ عَرَفَاتٍ فَاذْكُرُوا اللَّهَ عِنْدَ الْمَشْعَرِ الْحَرَامِ) [البقرة: 198] الآيَتَيْنِ.

وَيَدْعُو حَتَّى يُسْفِرَ جِدّاً ثُمَّ يَدْفَعُ إِلَى مِنَى، فَإِذَا بَلَغَ مُحَسِّراً أَسْرَعَ رَمْيَةَ حَجَرٍ، وَأَخَذَ حَصَى الجِمَارِ سَبْعِينَ حَصَاةً أَكْبَرَ مِنَ الحِمِّصِ وَدُونَ البُنْدُقِ، مِنْ حَيْثُ شَاءَ، وَكُرِهَ مِنَ الحَرَمِ، وَالحُشِّ، وَتَكْسِيرُهُ، وَلَا يُسَنُّ غَسْلُهُ، وَتُجْزِئُ حَصَاةٌ نَجِسَةٌ مَعَ الكَرَاهَةِ.

They then stone only Jamarat al-ʿAqabah with seven pebbles.

It is a prerequisite that they throw them one after the other and not merely place them down. With each pebble, they raise their right arm until the white of the armpit is seen and make takbīr. They then slaughter and shave or trim all their hair—not necessarily every single hair. Women are to trim the amount of a fingertip.

At this point, everything is now permitted besides women.

Then they go to Makkah and perform the visitation ṭawāf, a pillar, and make saʿī if they had not already done so. After concluding this, everything becomes permissible. It is recommended to drink zamzam water for whatever is desired, to fill the belly and sprinkle it on the body and clothes, and to supplicate from what is narrated.

فَيَرْمِي جَمْرَةَ العَقَبَةِ وَحْدَهَا بِسَبْعٍ، وَيُشْتَرَطُ الرَّمْيُ فَلَا يُجْزِئُ الوَضْعُ، وَكَوْنُهُ وَاحِدَةً بَعدَ أُخْرَى، يَرْفَعُ يُمْنَاهُ مَعَ كُلِّ حَصَاةٍ حَتَّى يُرَى بَيَاضُ إِبْطِهِ، وَيُكَبِّرُ مَعَ كُلِّ حَصَاةٍ، ثُمَّ يَنْحَرُ وَيَحْلِقُ أَوْ يُقَصِّرُ مِنْ جَمِيعِ شَعْرِهِ، لَا مِنْ كُلِّ شَعْرَةٍ بِعَيْنِهَا، وَالمَرْأَةُ تُقَصِّرُ مِنْ شَعْرِهَا قَدْرَ أَنْمُلَةٍ،

ثُمَّ قَدْ حَلَّ كُلَّ شَيْءٍ إِلَّا النِّسَاءَ، ثُمَّ يُفِيضُ إِلَى مَكَّةَ فَيَطُوفُ طَوَافَ الزِّيَارَةِ الَّذِي هُوَ رُكْنٌ، ثُمَّ يَسْعَى إِنْ لَمْ يَكُنْ سَعَى، وَقَدْ حَلَّ لَهُ كُلُّ شَيْءٍ.

وَسُنَّ أَنْ يَشْرَبَ مِنْ زَمْزَمَ لِمَا أَحَبَّ، وَيَتَضَلَّعُ وَيَرُشُّ عَلَى بَدَنِهِ وَثَوْبِهِ وَيَدْعُو بِمَا وَرَدَ.

Minā & Madīnah

They then return, on the day of naḥr[119], to Minā and pray ẓuhr, sleep there three nights, and during the days of tashrīq they stone the three jamarāts with seven pebbles each. Stoning is not valid unless done during the day after the zawāl; except by water-bearers and shepherds. If stoning was performed at night or before the zawāl it would not be valid. It is recommended to do it before ẓuhr prayer.

The farewell ṭawāf is obligatory and is to be done by everyone wishing to leave Makkah. Afterwards, they stop at the multazam (between the corner and the door) and cling to it with their entire body, supplicating with what is narrated. Women experiencing menstruation and postpartum bleeding are to supplicate at the door of the masjid.

It is recommended to enter the House unarmed and without khuffs or sandals.

It is recommended to visit the Prophet's grave ﷺ and the graves of his two companions ؓ. They should greet him with salām while facing him and then turn toward the qiblah with the house—impermissible to make ṭawāf around—on the left and supplicate.

The manner of ʿumrah for those in the sanctuary is to make iḥrām from the closest non-sacred area. Those closer than the miqāt do so from their home, otherwise it is made from it. It is permissible to make it numerous times in one year and is best done in the months besides those of ḥajj; Ramaḍān is most virtuous.

[119] The 10th of Dhul-Ḥijjah on which the pilgrims slaughter.

فَصْلٌ

ثُمَّ يَرْجِعُ فَيُصَلِّي ظُهْرَ يَوْمَ النَّحْرِ بِمِنَى، وَيَبِيتُ بِهَا ثَلَاثَ لَيَالٍ، وَيَرْمِي الجَمَرَاتِ الثَّلَاثَ بِهَا أَيَّامَ التَّشْرِيقِ، كُلَّ جَمْرَةٍ بِسَبْعِ حَصَيَاتٍ، وَلَا يُجْزِئُ رَمْيُ غَيْرِ سُقَاةٍ وَرُعَاةٍ إِلَّا نَهَاراً بَعْدَ الزَّوَالِ، فَإِنْ رَمَى لَيْلاً أَوْ قَبْلَ الزَّوَالِ لَمْ يُجْزِئْهُ، وَسُنَّ قَبْلَ صَلَاةِ الظُّهْرِ.

وَطَوَافُ الوَدَاعِ وَاجِبٌ يَفْعَلُهُ كُلُّ مَنْ أَرَادَ الخُرُوجَ مِنْ مَكَّةَ، ثُمَّ يَقِفُ فِي المُلْتَزَمِ بَيْنَ الرُّكْنِ وَالبَابِ مُلْصِقاً بِهِ جَمِيعَهُ دَاعِياً بِمَا وَرَدَ، وَتَدْعُو الحَائِضُ وَالنُّفَسَاءُ عَلَى بَابِ المَسْجِدِ.

وَسُنَّ دُخُولُهُ البَيْتَ بِلَا خُفٍّ وَلَا نَعْلٍ وَلَا سِلَاحٍ.

وَتُسْتَحَبُّ زِيَارَةُ قَبْرِ النَّبِيِّ ﷺ وَقَبْرَيْ صَاحِبَيْهِ رضي الله عنهما، فَيُسَلِّمُ عَلَيْهِ مُسْتَقْبِلاً لَهُ، ثُمَّ يَسْتَقْبِلُ القِبْلَةَ وَيَجْعَلُ الحُجْرَةَ عَنْ يَسَارِهِ وَيَدْعُو، وَيَحْرُمُ الطَّوَافُ بِهَا.

وَصِفَةُ العُمْرَةِ أَنْ يُحْرِمَ بِهَا مَنْ بِالحَرَمِ مِنْ أَدْنَى الحِلِّ، وَغَيْرُهُ مِنْ دُوَيْرَةِ أَهْلِهِ إِنْ كَانَ دُونَ مِيقَاتٍ وَإِلَّا فَمِنْهُ، وَلَا بَأْسَ بِهَا فِي السَّنَةِ مِرَاراً، وَهِيَ فِي غَيْرِ أَشْهُرِ الحَجِّ، وَفِي رَمَضَانَ أَفْضَلُ.

Pillars & Obligations of Ḥajj

Ḥajj has four pillars which are: iḥrām; wuqūf[120]; ṭawāf; and saʿī.

It has seven obligations which are: iḥrām from the miqāt; wuqūf until sunset (for those who stay in the day); staying in Muzdalifah until after midnight (for those who arrived before); staying overnight in Minā during the nights of tashrīq; stoning in sequence; shaving or trimming; and making the farewell ṭawāf.

ʿUmrah has three pillars which are: iḥrām; ṭawāf; and saʿī.

It has two obligations which are: making iḥrām from the miqāt; and shaving or trimming.

The recommended acts include the following: staying overnight at Minā on the night of ʿArafah; arrival ṭawāf; short-stride jogging; and tucking the top wrap under the right arm, etc. Ḥajj is not complete if a pillar is abandoned. Whoever abandons an obligation must offer a blood sacrifice and their ḥajj will be valid. Whoever abandons a recommended act is not required to do anything. Whoever misses the wuqūf at ʿArafah has missed the ḥajj and disengages to ʿumrah (which does not fulfill the obligatory ʿumrah) and slaughters if they did not make a condition. They are required to make it up the following year.

Whoever is prevented from the Kaʿbah, even if after the wuqūf or during ʿumrah, is obliged to slaughter the sacrificial animal with the intention of disengagement. If it is not available, they must fast 10 days with an intention[121], thus disengaging without a penalty of feeding. Whoever is prevented from ʿArafah during ḥajj is to disengage to ʿumrah without requirement of a blood sacrifice.

---

[120] Staying at ʿArafah.

[121] The intention is the same as slaughtering the sacrificial animal i.e. disengagement.

فَصْلٌ

أَرْكَانُ الحَجِّ أَرْبَعَةٌ: إِحْرَامٌ، وَوُقُوفٌ، وَطَوَافٌ، وَسَعْيٌ.

وَوَاجِبَاتُهُ سَبْعَةٌ: الإِحْرَامُ مِنْ المِيقَاتِ، وَوُقُوفُ مَنْ وَقَفَ نَهَاراً إِلَى الغُرُوبِ، وَالمَبِيتُ بِمُزْدَلِفَةَ إِلَى بَعْدَ نِصْفِ اللَّيْلِ إِنْ وَافَاهَا قَبْلَهُ، وَالمَبِيتُ بِمِنَى لَيَالِي التَّشْرِيقِ، وَالرَّمْيُ مُرَتَّباً، وَالحَلْقُ أَوْ التَّقْصِيرُ، وَطَوَافُ الوَدَاعِ.

وَأَرْكَانُ العُمْرَةِ ثَلَاثَةٌ: إِحْرَامٌ، وَطَوَافٌ، وَسَعْيٌ.

وَوَاجِبَاتُهَا شَيْئَانِ: الإِحْرَامُ مِنَ المِيقَاتِ، وَالحَلْقُ أَوْ التَّقْصِيرُ.

وَالمَسْنُونُ كَالمَبِيتِ بِمِنَى لَيْلَةَ عَرَفَةَ، وَطَوَافُ القُدُومِ، وَالرَّمَلُ، وَالاضْطِبَاعُ وَنَحْوُ ذَلِكَ.

فَمَنْ تَرَكَ رُكْناً لَمْ يَتِمَّ حَجُّهُ إِلَّا بِهِ، وَمَنْ تَرَكَ وَاجِباً فَعَلَيْهِ دَمٌ وَحَجُّهُ صَحِيحٌ، وَمَنْ تَرَكَ مَسْنُوناً فَلَا شَيْءَ عَلَيْهِ، وَمَنْ فَاتَهُ الوُقُوفُ بِعَرَفَةَ فَاتَهُ الحَجُّ، وَتَحَلَّلَ بِعُمْرَةٍ، وَلَا تُجْزِئُ عَنْ عُمْرَةِ الإِسْلَامِ، وَهَدَى إِنْ لَمْ يَكُنْ اِشْتَرَطَ، وَقَضَى مِنَ العَامِ القَابِلِ.

وَمَنْ مُنِعَ البَيْتَ وَلَوْ بَعْدَ الوُقُوفِ أَوْ فِي عُمْرَةٍ ذَبَحَ هَدْياً بِنِيَّةِ التَحَلُّلِ وُجُوباً، فَإِنْ لَمْ يَجِدْ صَامَ عَشَرَةَ أَيَّامٍ بِالنِّيَّةِ وَحَلَّ، وَلَا إِطْعَامَ فِيهِ، وَمَنْ صُدَّ عَنْ عَرَفَةَ فِي حَجٍّ تَحَلَّلَ بِعُمْرَةٍ وَلَا دَمَ عَلَيْهِ.

Hady, Uḍḥiyah & ʿAqīqah

The hady is livestock, etc., which is offered to the sanctuary because it is offered to Allāh. The uḍḥiyah is an eligible camel, cow, or sheep that is slaughtered during the days of naḥr, for the ʿEid[123], as an act of devotion to Allāh. It is an emphasized recommended act and obligatory due to an oath. The most virtuous is a camel, followed by a cow, and then a sheep. It is not valid with other animals. One sheep is sufficient for a man, his dependents, and family. A camel or cow is sufficient for seven and is considered a slaughter on their behalf. One sheep is better than one-seventh of a camel or cow and seven sheep are better than one of the others.

It is not valid except with a six-month-old male sheep or a thaniy of something else. A thaniy camel is a five-year-old and a thaniy cow is a two-year-old. The emaciated, clearly one-eyed, hobbled, or one missing its front teeth, most of its ear, or horn, will not suffice.

It is recommended to slaughter a camel, standing with its left leg bound, by puncturing the pit between its neck and sternum. The slaughtering of a cow and sheep is done, laying on their left side, while facing the qiblah. It is obligatory to mention Allāh's name at the onset of slaughter. Takbīr is made and the following is said, "O Allāh this is from You and for You".

The time to slaughter an uḍḥiyah, oath-hady or voluntary sacrifice, mutʿah, and qirān, is after the earliest ʿEid prayer of the area (or its equivalent for those who do not pray[124]). If the prayer is missed (due to the zawāl), slaughter is to commence after it and continue until the second day of tashrīq. The time to slaughter an obligatory hady is upon committing the unlawful.

---

123 The time for slaughter is from the conclusion of ʿEīd prayer until the end of the second day after it.

124 Like someone who lives in a remote area where ʿEīd prayers are not offered.

فَصْلٌ فِي الهَدْيِ وَالأُضْحِيَةِ وَالعَقِيقَةِ

الهَدْيُ مَا يُهْدَى لِلْحَرَمِ مِنْ نَعَمٍ وَغَيْرِهِ؛ لِأَنَّهُ يُهْدَى إِلَى اللهِ تَعَالَى.

وَالأُضْحِيَةُ مَا يُذْبَحُ مِنْ إِبِلٍ وَبَقَرٍ وَغَنَمٍ أَهْلِيَّةٍ أَيَّامَ النَّحْرِ بِسَبَبِ العِيْدِ تَقَرُّباً إِلَى اللهِ تَعَالَى، وَهِيَ سُنَّةٌ مُؤَكَّدَةٌ، وَتَجِبُ بِالنُّذُورِ، وَالأَفْضَلُ إِبِلٌ فَبَقَرٌ فَغَنَمٌ، وَلَا تُجْزِئُ مِنْ غَيْرِهِنَّ، وَتُجْزِئُ شَاةٌ عَنْ وَاحِدٍ وَأَهْلِ بَيْتِهِ وَعِيَالِهِ، وَبَدَنَةٌ أَوْ بَقَرَةٌ عَنْ سَبْعَةٍ، وَيُعْتَبَرُ ذَبْحُهَا عَنْهُمْ، وَشَاةٌ أَفْضَلُ مِنْ سُبْعِ بَدَنَةٍ أَوْ بَقَرَةٍ، وَسَبْعُ شِيَاهٍ أَفْضَلُ مِنْ إِحْدَاهُمَا.

وَلَا يُجْزِئُ إِلَّا جَذَعُ ضَأْنٍ أَوْ ثَنِيُّ غَيْرِهِ، فَثَنِيُّ إِبِلٍ مَا لَهُ خَمْسُ سِنِينَ، وَثَنِيُّ بَقَرٍ مَا لَهُ سَنَتَانِ، وَلَا تُجْزِئُ هَزِيلَةٌ وَبَيِّنَةُ عَوَرٍ أَوْ عَرَجٍ، وَلَا ذَاهِبَةُ الثَّنَايَا أَوْ أَكْثَرِ أُذُنِهَا أَوْ قَرْنِهَا.

وَسُنَّ نَحْرُ إِبِلٍ قَائِمَةً مَعْقُولَةً يَدُهَا اليُسْرَى بِأَنْ يَطْعَنَهَا فِي الوَهْدَةِ بَيْنَ العُنُقِ وَالصَّدْرِ، وَذَبْحُ بَقَرٍ وَغَنَمٍ عَلَى جَنْبِهَا الأَيْسَرِ مُوَجَّهَةً إِلَى القِبْلَةِ، وَيُسَمِّي وُجُوباً حِيْنَ يُحَرِّكُ يَدَهُ بِالفِعْلِ وَيُكَبِّرُ وَيَقُولُ: اللَّهُمَّ هَذَا مِنْكَ وَلَكَ.

وَوَقْتُ ذَبْحِ أُضْحِيَةٍ وَهَدْيِ نَذْرٍ أَوْ تَطَوُّعٍ وَمُتْعَةٍ وَقِرَانٍ مِنْ بَعْدِ أَسْبَقِ صَلَاةِ العِيدِ بِالبَلَدِ أَوْ قَدْرِهَا لِمَنْ لَمْ يُصَلِّ، فَإِنْ فَاتَتْ الصَّلَاةُ بِالزَّوَالِ ذَبَحَ بَعْدَهُ إِلَى آخِرِ ثَانِي التَّشْرِيقِ، وَوَقْتُ ذَبْحِ هَدْيٍ وَاجِبٍ بِفِعْلٍ مَحْظُورٍ مِنْ حِينِهِ.

Distribution of Hady

The hady is specified by saying, “this is a hady”, by a garland tie, or a blood-marking. The uḍḥiyah is specified by saying, “with this uḍḥiyah” or “for Allāh”, etc.

It is not permitted to give the butcher his wages from it, though it is permitted as a gift or charity. No part of it, including its skin, is to be sold; rather, it is to be used.

It is recommended to divide it into the following three parts: to eat, to give as a gift, and to distribute as charity. It is recommended to eat from the voluntary hady and uḍḥiyah,even if obligatory. It is also permitted for the mutʿah and qirān. It is obligatory to give what is defined as meat in charity, which is considered property of the impoverished and, thus, it is not enough to simply feed them.

When the 10 begin, it is impermissible for those who are offering an uḍḥiyah (or having one offered on their behalf) to remove any hair, nails, or skin until the slaughter. It is recommended to shave afterward.

فَصْلٌ

وَيَتَعَيَّنُ هَدْيٌ بِقَوْلِهِ: هَذَا هَدْيٌ، أَوْ بِتَقْلِيدِهِ أَوْ إِشْعَارِهِ، وَأُضْحِيَةٌ: بِهَذِهِ أُضْحِيَةٌ أَوْ لِلَّهِ وَنَحْوِهِ.

وَلَا يَجُوزُ إِعْطَاءُ الجَازِرِ أُجْرَتَهُ مِنْهَا، وَيَجُوزُ هَدِيَّةً وَصَدَقَةً، وَلَا يُبَاعُ جِلْدُهَا، وَلَا شَيْءٌ مِنْهَا؛ بَلْ يَنْتَفِعُ بِهِ.

وَسُنَّ أَنْ يَأْكُلَ وَيُهْدِيَ وَيَتَصَدَّقَ أَثْلَاثاً، وَأَنْ يَأْكُلَ مِنْ هَدْيِهِ التَّطَوُّعِ، وَمِنْ أُضْحِيَتِهِ وَلَوْ وَاجِبَةً، وَيَجُوزُ مِنْ المُتْعَةِ وَالقِرَانِ، وَيَجِبُ أَنْ يَتَصَدَّقَ بِمَا يَقَعُ عَلَيْهِ اسْمُ اللَّحْمِ، وَيُعْتَبَرُ تَمْلِيكٌ لِلْفَقِيرِ، فَلَا يَكْفِي إِطْعَامُهُ.

وَإِذَا دَخَلَ العَشْرُ حَرُمَ عَلَى مَنْ يُضَحِّي أَوْ يُضَحَّى عَنْهُ أَخْذُ شَيْءٍ مِنْ شَعْرِهِ أَوْ ظُفْرِهِ أَوْ بَشَرَتِهِ إِلَى الذَّبْحِ، وَسُنَّ حَلْقٌ بَعْدَهُ.

ʿAqīqah

The ʿaqīqah is an emphasized recommended act for the father. For a boy, two sheep similar in age and appearance are offered. If both are unavailable, one will suffice. For a girl, one sheep is offered. A she-camel or cow will not suffice, unless offered entirely and slaughtered on the seventh day after birth, on which the child should be named. If that opportunity is missed, then the 14th, and then the 21st if it is missed again. The following weeks after that are not to be considered.

Its bones are not to be broken. It is better to cook it and include something sweet. Its ruling is like the uḍḥiyah in regard to what is sufficient, recommended, and disliked, though its skin, head, and discarded remains can be sold to give their value in charity. If the time for an ʿaqīqah and uḍḥiyah coincide, one will suffice the other.

فَصْلٌ

وَالعَقِيقَةُ سُنَّةٌ مُؤَكَّدَةٌ فِي حَقِّ الأَبِ، وَهِيَ عَنْ الغُلَامِ شَاتَانِ مُتَقَارِبَتَانِ سِنّاً وَشَبَهاً، فَإِنْ عُدِمَ فَوَاحِدَةٌ، وَعَنْ الجَارِيَةِ شَاةٌ، وَلَا يُجْزِئُ بَدَنَةٌ أَوْ بَقَرَةٌ إِلَّا كَامِلَةً تُذْبَحُ فِي سَابِعِ وِلَادَتِهِ وَيُسَمَّى فِيهِ، فَإِنْ فَاتَ فَفِي أَرْبَعَةَ عَشَرَ، فَإِنْ فَاتَ فَفِي أَحَدٍ وَعِشْرِينَ، وَلَا تُعْتَبَرُ الأَسَابِيعُ بَعْدَ ذَلِكَ.

وَلَا يُكْسَرُ عَظْمُهَا، وَطَبْخُهَا أَفْضَلُ، وَيَكُونُ مِنْهُ بِحُلْوٍ، وَحُكْمُهَا كَأُضْحِيَةٍ فِيمَا يُجْزِئُ وَيُسْتَحَبُّ وَيُكْرَهُ، لَكِنْ يُبَاعُ جِلْدٌ وَرَأْسٌ وَسَوَاقِطُ، وَيُتَصَدَّقُ بِثَمَنِهِ، وَإِنْ اتَّفَقَ وَقْتُ عَقِيقَةٍ وَأُضْحِيَةٍ أَجْزَأَتْ إِحْدَاهُمَا عَنْ الأُخْرَى.

Military Service

It is a communal obligation unless the enemy is present, has surrounded someone or their land, or there is a general mobilization upon which it becomes an individual obligation.

When it is already sufficiently fulfilled, it is an emphasized recommended act. It is not obligatory, except upon free healthy Muslim men of legal capacity. It is the most virtuous voluntary deed. Naval expeditions are preferred.

It is recommended to stand guard for at least one hour by manning the fortified borderline of combat; 40 days is a complete term. It is most preferred in the presence of severe fear and is better than residing in Makkah.

An insolvent debtor is not to voluntarily enlist without permission, acquired collateral, or a solvent guarantor; nor is someone with at least one of their parents, who is a free Muslim, to enlist without their permission.

It is not permitted for the Muslims to flee from an army that is twice their size even if it is one-on-two. If they are more than twice their size, it is permitted.

It is not permissible to kill children; women; hermaphrodites; priests; decrepit, old, or chronically ill men; or the blind who do not provide counsel for them and are not able to fight or abet.

Regarding captured free soldiers, the commander-in-chief must choose between execution, serfdom, releasing, or ransoming them in exchange for either a Muslim or wealth. It is obligatory that he makes the most appropriate choice and, if in doubt, execution is most suitable.

كِتَابُ الجِهَادِ

وَهُوَ فَرْضُ كِفَايَةٍ، إِلَّا إِذَا حَضَرَهُ أَوْ حَصَرَهُ أَوْ بَلَدَهُ عَدُوٌّ، أَوْ كَانَ النَّفِيرُ عَامًّا فَفَرْضُ عَيْنٍ.

وَيُسَنُّ بِتَأَكُّدٍ مَعَ قِيَامِ مَنْ يَكْفِي بِهِ، وَلَا يَجِبُ إِلَّا عَلَى ذَكَرٍ مُسْلِمٍ، حُرٍّ، مُكَلَّفٍ، صَحِيحٍ، وَأَفْضَلُ مُتَطَوَّعٍ بِهِ الجِهَادُ، وَغَزْوُ البَحْرِ أَفْضَلُ.

وَسُنَّ رِبَاطٌ، وَهُوَ لُزُومُ ثَغْرٍ لِجِهَادٍ، وَلَوْ سَاعَةً، وَتَمَامُهُ أَرْبَعُونَ يَوْماً، وَأَفْضَلُهُ بِأَشَدِّ خَوْفٍ، وَهُوَ أَفْضَلُ مِنَ المَقَامِ بِمَكَّةَ.

وَلَا يَتَطَوَّعُ بِهِ مَدِينٌ لَا وَفَاءَ لَهُ، إِلَّا مَعَ إِذْنٍ أَوْ رَهْنٍ مُحْرِزٍ أَوْ كَفِيلٍ مَلِيءٍ، وَلَا مَنْ أَحَدُ أَبَوَيْهِ حُرٌّ مُسْلِمٌ إِلَّا بِإِذْنِهِ.

وَلَا يَحِلُّ لِلْمُسْلِمِينَ الفِرَارُ مِنْ مِثْلَيْهِمْ وَلَوْ وَاحِداً مِن اثْنَيْنِ، فَإِنْ زَادُوا عَلَى مِثْلَيْهِمْ جَازَ.

وَلَا يَجُوزُ قَتْلُ صَبِيٍّ، وَأُنْثَى وَخُنْثَى، وَرَاهِبٍ، وَشَيْخٍ فَانٍ، وَزَمِنٍ، وَأَعْمَى، لَا رَأْيَ لَهُمْ، وَلَمْ يُقَاتِلُوا أَوْ يُحَرِّضُوا عَلَى القِتَالِ.

وَيُخَيَّرُ الإِمَامُ فِي أَسِيرٍ حُرٍّ مُقَاتِلٍ بَيْنَ قَتْلٍ وَرِقٍّ وَمَنٍّ وَفِدَاءٍ بِمُسْلِمٍ أَوْ بِمَالٍ، وَيَجِبُ عَلَيْهِ اخْتِيَارُ الأَصْلَحِ، فَإِنْ تَرَدَّدَ نَظَرُهُ، فَقَتْلٌ أَوْلَى.

Recruitment & Spoils

It is required that the commander-in-chief and the army purify their intentions for Allāh in their acts of obedience. At the time of expedition, he is obliged to enter a contract with the soldiers and their steeds and prohibit whoever is not suitable for war, including discouragers, alarmists, intelligence agents, known hypocrites, inciters of civil unrest, children, and women (besides the elderly who serve as a water-bearers etc.).

It is impermissible to seek assistance from non-believers, except in dire need. He is to prevent his army from what is impermissible and from being occupied with commerce. He should prepare wages and gifts for the enduring soldiers and should seek counsel from the insightful.

Whoever kills a combatant during battle is allowed their spoils, which include clothing; jewelry; weaponry; his transport upon which he was fighting; and whatever is on it. His money, saddle, tent, and pack animal are considered war booty.

فَصْلٌ

وَيَلْزَمُ الإِمَامَ وَالجَيْشَ إِخْلَاصُ النِّيَةِ لِلَّهِ تَعَالَى فِي الطَّاعَاتِ، وَعَلَيْهِ عِنْدَ المَسِيرِ تَعَاهُدُ الرِّجَالِ وَالخَيْلِ، وَمَنْعُ مَنْ لَا يَصْلُحُ لِلْحَرْبِ، وَمُخَذِّلٍ وَمُرْجِفٍ، وَمُكَاتِبٍ بِأَخْبَارِنَا وَمَعْرُوفٍ بِنِفَاقٍ، وَرَامٍ بَيْنَنَا بِفِتَنٍ، وَصَبِيٍّ وَنِسَاءٍ إِلَّا عَجُوزاً لِسَقْيِ مَاءٍ وَنَحْوِهِ.

وَيَحْرُمُ اسْتِعَانَةٌ بِكَافِرٍ إِلَّا لِضَرُورَةٍ، وَيَمْنَعُ جَيْشَهُ مِنْ مُحَرَّمٍ، وَتَشَاغُلٍ بِتِجَارَةٍ، وَيَعِدُ الصَّابِرَ بِأَجْرٍ وَنَفْلٍ، وَيُشَاوِرُ ذَا رَأْيٍ.

وَمَنْ قَتَلَ قَتِيلاً فِي حَالَةِ الحَرْبِ فَلَهُ سَلَبُهُ وَهُوَ مَا عَلَيْهِ مِنْ ثِيَابٍ وَحُلِيٍّ وَسِلَاحٍ، وَكَذَا دَابَّتُهُ الَّتِي قَاتَلَ عَلَيْهَا، وَمَا عَلَيْهَا، وَأَمَّا نَفَقَتُهُ وَرَحْلُهُ وَخَيْمَتُهُ وَجَنِيبُهُ فَغَنِيمَةٌ.

Booty

Booty is acquired in battle territories by laying hold of it. One-fifth of it is divided into five shares, given to the following: Allāh and His messenger ﷺ (to be spent like fay'); the relatives i.e. the offspring of Hāshim and al-Muṭṭalib; the destitute orphan; the impoverished; and the wayfarer. The remainder is divided between anyone who attended the battle to fight etc. The foot soldiers are allotted one, the cavalrymen riding Arabian steeds are allotted three, while others are allotted two. Shares are not to be given for more than two steeds, nor for other riding beasts.

The following four prerequisites are required of whomever receives shares: puberty; sanity; freedom; and being male. If they do not meet even one prerequisite, they are given a paltry gift which is less than a share.

If a land is conquered in battle, the commander-in-chief is to choose between dividing it or endowing it to the Muslims via permanent land tax collection from whoever owns it.

Whatever money is collected from a non-believer without fighting, e.g. jizyah[126], land tax, 10% commerce tax from a ḥarbī[127], half of that from a dhimī[128], what they abandoned in fear, or that of the deceased with no inheritors is all fay' and to be spent to benefit the Muslim community.

---

[126] Tax collected to secure their safety and residency in the Muslim lands.

[127] Any non-Muslim that does not enjoy a pact, protection, or guarantee from the Muslim state.

[128] Anyone who pays the jizyah and is required to adhere to the laws of Islām due to their acknowledged disbelief.

فَصْلٌ

وَتُمْلَكُ الغَنِيمَةُ بِالاسْتِيلَاءِ عَلَيْهَا فِي دَارِ الحَرْبِ، فَيُجْعَلُ خُمُسُهَا خَمْسَةَ أَسْهُمٍ: لِلَّهِ وَرَسُولِهِ، يُصْرَفُ مَصْرِفَ الفَيْءِ، وَسَهْمٌ لِذَوِي القُرْبَى وَهُمْ بَنُو هَاشِمٍ وَالمُطَّلِبِ، وَسَهْمٌ لِلْيَتَامَى الفُقَرَاءِ، وَسَهْمٌ لِلْمَسَاكِينِ، وَسَهْمٌ لِأَبْنَاءِ السَّبِيلِ، ثُمَّ يُقَسَّمُ البَاقِي بَيْنَ مَنْ شَهِدَ الوَقْعَةَ لِقَصْدِ قِتَالٍ وَنَحْوِهِ: لِلرَّاجِلِ سَهْمٌ، وَلِلْفَارِسِ عَلَى فَرَسٍ عَرَبِيٍّ ثَلَاثَةٌ وَعَلَى غَيْرِهِ اثْنَانِ، وَلَا يُسْهَمُ لِأَكْثَرَ مِنْ فَرَسَيْنِ وَلَا لِغَيْرِ الخَيْلِ.

وَشُرِطَ فِيمَنْ يُسْهَمُ لَهُ أَرْبَعَةُ شُرُوطٍ: البُلُوغُ، وَالعَقْلُ، وَالحُرِّيَّةُ، وَالذُّكُورَةُ. فَإِنْ اخْتَلَّ شَرْطٌ رَضَخَ لَهُ وَلَمْ يُسْهِمْ، وَالرَّضْخُ العَطَاءُ دُونَ السَّهْمِ.

وَإِذَا فَتَحُوا أَرْضاً بِالسَّيْفِ خُيِّرَ الإِمَامُ بَيْنَ قَسْمِهَا وَوَقْفِهَا عَلَى المُسْلِمِينَ، ضَارِباً عَلَيْهَا خَرَاجاً مُسْتَمِراً يُؤْخَذُ مِمَّنْ هِيَ فِي يَدِهِ.

وَمَا أُخِذَ مِنْ مَالِ مُشْرِكٍ بِلَا قِتَالٍ كَجِزْيَةٍ، وَخَرَاجٍ، وَعُشْرِ تِجَارَةٍ مِنَ الحَرْبِيِّ، وَنِصْفِهِ مِنَ الذِّمِّيِّ، وَمَا تَرَكُوهُ فَزَعاً، أَوْ عَنْ مَيِّتٍ وَلَا وَارِثَ لَهُ، فَيْءٌ، وَمَصْرِفُهُ فِي مَصَالِحِ المُسْلِمِينَ.

Pacts

Pacts of protection are permitted with people who have a book, or something like a book, e.g. the Magians. The pact is not valid unless it is made by the ruler or his deputy.

It is obligatory if he is secure from their deceit and they conform to the following four rules: to willingly pay the jizyah, while they are humbled; to not mention Islām, except in a positive light; to refrain from doing anything that will bring about harm to the Muslims; and to apply the laws of Islām personally, financially, and as it pertains to dignity, (i.e. the legal penalty for what they have prohibited, like adultery, is applied but not for what they have permitted, like alcohol). The jizyah is not taken from a child, bondsman, woman, or the incapable destitute, etc.

They are required to distinguish themselves from the Muslims and are prohibited from riding steeds, carrying arms, and constructing buildings which tower over Muslims (even if they approve), which must be demolished. The dhimī is liable for what is destroyed (unless they have purchased it from a Muslim) and it is not to be reconstructed tall, even if they collapse, unless a Muslim has constructed a home in their district that is shorter than their structures.

They are not permitted to construct churches, reconstruct them if they collapse, publicize evil, holidays, crosses, eating and drinking during the daylight of Ramaḍān, swine, raise their voices for the deceased, recite the Qur'ān, ring bells, publicize their book, or buy a copy of the Qur'ān, books of Islamic Law or Prophetic Tradition. The ruler must protect them and prevent whoever would harm them.

فَصْلٌ

وَيَجُوزُ عَقْدُ الذِّمَّةِ لِمَنْ لَهُ كِتَابٌ أَوْ شِبْهَةُ كِتَابٍ كَالمَجُوسِ، وَلَا يَصِحُّ عَقْدُهَا إِلَّا مِنْ إِمَامٍ أَوْ نَائِبِهِ.

وَيَجِبُ إِنْ أَمِنَ مَكْرَهُمْ وَالْتَزَمُوا لَنَا بِأَرْبَعَةِ أَحْكَامٍ: أَنْ يُعْطُوا الجِزْيَةَ عَنْ يَدٍ وَهُمْ صَاغِرُونَ، وَأَنْ لَا يَذْكُرُوا دِينَ الإِسْلَامِ إِلَّا بِخَيْرٍ، وَأَنْ لَا يَفْعَلُوا مَا فِيهِ ضَرَرٌ عَلَى المُسْلِمِينَ، وَأَنْ تَجْرِيَ عَلَيْهِمْ أَحْكَامُ الإِسْلَامِ فِي نَفْسٍ وَمَالٍ وَعِرْضٍ وَإِقَامَةِ حَدٍّ فِيمَا يُحَرِّمُونَهُ كَالزِّنَا لَا فِيمَا يُحَلُّونَهُ كَالخَمْرِ، وَلَا تُؤْخَذُ الجِزْيَةُ مِنْ صَبِيٍّ وَعَبْدٍ وَامْرَأَةٍ وَفَقِيرٍ عَاجِزٍ عَنْهَا وَنَحْوِهِمْ.

وَيَلْزَمُهُمْ التَّمْيِيزُ عَنْ المُسْلِمِينَ، وَيُمْنَعُونَ مِنْ رُكُوبِ الخَيْلِ، وَحَمْلِ السِّلَاحِ، وَتَعْلِيَةِ بِنَاءٍ عَلَى مُسْلِمٍ وَلَوْ رَضِيَ، وَيَجِبُ نَقْضُهُ، وَيَضْمَنُ ذِمِّيٌّ مَا تَلِفَ بِهِ لَا إِنْ مَلَكُوهُ مِنْ مُسْلِمٍ، وَلَا يُعَادُ عَالِيًا لَوْ انْهَدَمَ، وَلَا إِنْ بَنَى مُسْلِمٌ دَارًا عِنْدَهُمْ دُونَ بِنَائِهِمْ.

وَمِنْ إِحْدَاثِ كَنَائِسَ، وَبِنَاءِ مَا انْهَدَمَ مِنْهَا، وَمِنْ إِظْهَارِ مُنْكَرٍ وَعِيدٍ وَصَلِيبٍ، وَأَكْلٍ وَشُرْبٍ نَهَارَ رَمَضَانَ، وَخَمْرٍ، وَخِنْزِيرٍ، وَرَفْعِ صَوتٍ عَلَى مَيِّتٍ، وَقِرَاءَةِ قُرْآنٍ، وَنَاقُوسٍ، وَجَهْرٍ بِكِتَابِهِمْ، وَشِرَاءِ مُصْحَفٍ وَفِقْهٍ وَحَدِيثٍ، وَعَلَى الإِمَامِ حِفْظُهُمْ، وَمَنْعُ مَنْ يُؤْذِيهِمْ.

Breaking Pacts

Whoever refuses to pay the jizyah, be humble, adhere to our law or fights us, commits adultery with a Muslim woman or lays with her under the banner of marriage, commits highway robbery, spies or houses a spy, mentions Allāh, His book, His religion, or His messenger ﷺ in an evil way, transgresses a Muslim by killing them or causing them confusion in their faith will have their (but not their family's) pact broken. The ruler must treat them like a captive combatant and choose what to do with them. Their wealth becomes fay'; however, it is impermissible to kill them if they accept Islām, even having cursed the Prophet ﷺ.

فَصْلٌ

وَمَنْ أَبَى مِنْهُمْ بَذْلَ الجِزْيَةِ، أَوْ الصَّغَارَ، أَوْ الْتِزَامَ حُكْمِنا، أَوْ قَاتَلَنَا أَوْ زَنَا بِمُسْلِمَةٍ، أَوْ أَصَابَهَا بِاسْمِ نِكَاحٍ، أَوْ قَطَعَ الطَّرِيقَ أَوْ تَجَسَّسَ، أَوْ آوَى جَاسُوساً، أَوْ ذَكَرَ اللَّهَ تَعَالَى وَكِتَابَهُ، أَوْ دِينَهُ، أَوْ رَسُولَهُ بِسُوءٍ، أَوْ تَعَدَّى عَلَى مُسْلِمٍ بِقَتْلٍ أَوْ فِتْنَةٍ عَنْ دِينِهِ انْتَقَضَ عَهْدُهُ دُونَ ذُرِّيَّتِهِ، فَيُخَيَّرُ الإِمَامُ فِيهِ كَالأَسِيرِ الحَرْبِيِّ، وَمَالُهُ فَيْءٌ، فَيَحْرُمُ قَتْلُهُ إِنْ أَسْلَمَ، وَلَوْ كَانَ سَبَّ النَّبِيَّ ﷺ.

Conclusion

With the success and aid of Allāh, this is the last of what was easy to collect. All praise belongs to Allāh, the Lord of the worlds, and may abundant peace and prayers be upon our leader Muḥammad, his family, and companions.

In need of His Lord, The Sufficient Benefactor's pardon and forgiveness, Abu Abd Allāh ʿAbd al-Raḥmān b. Aḥmad b. Muḥammad b. Aḥmad b. Muḥammad b. Muṣṭafā al-Ḥanbali al-Khalwati al-Qādiri, the resident of Aleppo from Damascus, may Allāh pardon his sins and cover his faults and those of his Muslim brothers, completed his work Monday afternoon on the 17th of Jumādā al-Ulā, 1159. May peace, pleasure, and prayers be upon our leader Muḥammad, his family, and companions.

خاتمةُ الكِتَابِ

وَهَذَا آخِرُ مَا تَيَسَّرَ جَمْعُهُ بِتَوْفِيقِ اللَّهِ تَعَالَى وَمَعُونَتِهِ، وَصَلَّى اللَّهُ عَلَى سَيِّدِنَا مُحَمَّدٍ وَعَلَى آلِهِ وَصَحْبِهِ وَسَلَّمَ تَسْلِيماً كَثِيراً، وَالحَمْدُ لِلَّهِ رَبِّ العَالَمِينَ.

وَفَرَغَ مِنْ تَأْلِيفِهِ كَاتِبُهُ فَقِيرُ العَفْوِ وَالغُفْرَانِ مِنْ رَبِّهِ الغَنِيِّ المَنَّانِ: أَبُو عَبْدِ اللَّهِ عَبْدُ الرَّحْمَنِ بْنُ عَبْدِ اللَّهِ بْنِ أَحْمَدَ بْنِ مُحَمَّدِ بْنِ أَحْمَدَ بْنِ مُحَمَّدِ بْنِ مُصْطَفَى الحَنْبَلِيُّ مَذْهَباً، الخَلْوَتِيُّ ثُمَّ القَادِرِيُّ مَشْرَباً، الدِّمَشْقِيُّ مَوْلِداً، الحَلَبِيُّ مَحْتِداً، غَفَرَ اللَّهُ لَهُ مَا كَانَ مِنَ الذُّنُوبِ، وَسَتَرَ مَا شَانَ مِنَ العُيُوبِ، وَلِإِخْوَانِهِ المُسْلِمِينَ، إِنَّهُ أَكْرَمُ الأَكْرَمِينَ، وَأَرْحَمُ الرَّاحِمِينَ، عَصْرَ الاثْنَيْنِ المُبَارَكِ السَّابِعَ عَشَرَ مِنْ جُمَادَى الأُولَى مِنْ سَنَةِ تِسْعٍ وَخَمْسِينَ وَمِائَةٍ وَأَلْفٍ، وَصَلَّى اللَّهُ عَلَى سَيِّدِنَا مُحَمَّدٍ وَعَلَى آلِهِ وَصَحْبِهِ، وَالسَّلَامُ وَالرِّضَا عَلَيْهِ وَعَلَيْهِمْ أَجْمَعِينَ.

Bibliography

Al lafi, T., & Ababneh, H. (1995). The effect of the extract of the miswak (chewing sticks) used in Jordan and the Middle East on oral bacteria. *International Dental Journal*, 218-222.

al-Bali, A. a.-R. (1997). *Bidayat al-Abid wa Kifayat al-Zahid.* Beirut: Dar al-Basha'ir al-Islamiya.

al-Bali, A. a.-R. (2000). *Bulugh al-Qasid Jull al-Maqasid.* Beirut: Dar al-Basha'ir al-Islamiyyah.

al-Bali, A. a.-R. (2002). *Kashf al-Mukhadarat wa al-Riyad al-Muzharat.* Beirut: Dar al-Basha'ir al-Islamiyyah.

al-Buhuti, M. Y. (1983). *Kashshaf al-Qina' an Matn al-Iqna.* Beirut: Alim al-Kutub.

al-Buhuti, M. Y. (1993). *Daqa'iq Uli al-Naha li Sharh al-Muntaha.* Beirut: Alim al-Kutub.

Ali, A. Y. (1946). *The Holy Qur-an. Text, Translation and Commentary.* Doha: Qatar National Printing Press.

al-Jawziyyah, M. A. (1991). *I'lam al-Muwaqqi'in 'an Rabb al-'Alimin.* Beirut: Dar al-Kutub al-Ilmiyah.

al-Karamy, M. Y. (2004). *Dalil al-Talib li Nayl al-Ma'arib.* Riyadh: Dar Tayyibah.

al-Kurdy, D. M.-D. (2005). *al-Maqadir al-Shariyyah wa al-Ahkam al-Fiqhiyyah al-Mutaliqah biha.* Cairo.

al-Maqdasi, A. A. (1968). *Al-Mughni.* Cairo: Maktabat al-Qahirah.

al-Mardawi, A. a.-D. (1994). *Al-Insaf fi Ma'rifat al-Rajih min al-Khilaf.* Cairo: Hajar.

Bahjat, A. (2016). Nadhm al-Maqadir al-Shariah bil Wihdat al-Muasirah. Madinah, KSA.

Jung, D. (2011). *The Value of Agarwood: Reflections upon its use and history in South Yemen.* Germany: Universitätsbibliothel, Universität Heidelberg.

Management of Acute Abnormal Uterine Bleeding in Nonpregnant Reproductive-Aged Women. (2013). *The*

American College of Obstetricians and Gynecologists, 891-896.

Philip Zeplin, M. M. (2016). Clitoral Hood Reduction. *Aesthetic Surgery Journal*, 36-37.

Qalajy, M., & Hamid Qunaiby. (1988). *Mu'jam Lughat al-Fuqaha'*. Beirut: Dar al-Nafa'is.

Qasim, A. a.-R. (1977). *Hashiyat al-Rawd al-Murbi' Sharh Zad al-Mustaqni*. Riyadh.

Revenig, L., Leung, A., & Hsiao, W. (2014). Ejaculatory Physiology and Pathophysiology: Assessment and Treatment in Male Infertility. *Translational Andrology and Urology*, 31-39.

Uthaimeen, M. S. (2007). *al-Sharh al-Mumti ala Zad al-Mustaqni*. Cairo: Dar Ibn al-Jawzy.

About the Translator

Abu Ibrāhīm John Starling is an alumnus of NCSU's Poole College of Management and the Islamic University of Madinah. He holds a master's degree in Islamic Studies from the Islamic University of Minnesota and possesses traditional ijazahs in several subjects including Ḥanbali fiqh from Shaykh, Dr. Muṭlaq al-Jāsir. He is an avid student of the Islamic sciences and has sought knowledge both formally and traditionally since 2001.

Notes:

Made in the USA
Middletown, DE
27 July 2020

13699958R00106